Barb
you are great!

Magnificent Surrender

Magnificent Surrender

Releasing the Riches of Living in the Lord

ROGER B. HELLAND

WIPF & STOCK · Eugene, Oregon

MAGNIFICENT SURRENDER
Releasing the Riches of Living in the Lord

Wipf & Stock
An Imprint of Wipf and Stock Publishers
199 W. 8th Ave., Suite 3
Eugene, OR 97401
www.wipfandstock.com

ISBN 13: 978-1-61097-733-3
Manufactured in the U.S.A.

Contents

Acknowledgments

WINSTON CHURCHILL REFLECTED, "WRITING a book is an adventure. To begin with, it is a toy and an amusement. Then it becomes a master, and then it becomes a tyrant." For three quarters of 2011, this book ruled my heart and any free time that I could find, off and on, between work and family priorities. This is my fifth volume; writing never seems to get easier. It's been an adventure of labor and love, driven by a passion to communicate Colossians and Christ to others. I owe a debt of gratitude to many people whose ideas or involvement assisted me on the way.

To the late Dr. Stanley Grenz who incited my value for theological reflection in life and leadership and who modeled a lively balance between scholarship and practice. I've tried to model that in this book. To Drs. Douglas Moo and N.T. Wright, whose commentaries on Colossians were steady companions that I regularly consulted as exegetical guides.

To Mrs. Sandy Derksen—my daughter's mother-in-law, and a dear friend—who provided meticulous copy-editing and proofreading for the final draft as she double-checked all Scripture references, and helped repair any bad grammar and style. To friends Mrs. Laurie Rolfe in Colorado, and Mrs. Cathy Byers in Thailand, who donated their precious time to read parts of the early draft and offered insightful comments that helped clarify and expand the content in ways that made the book more accessible. To a leading lady, Mrs. Lorna Rande, a long-time friend in British Columbia, who read the entire manuscript and pointed out the tiniest of mistakes as she also proposed numerous gracious suggestions, which improved the final result.

To my editor Mr. Christian Amondson, for his speedy email replies and answers to my questions, and for his professionalism that helped me get this book published in a timely fashion.

And finally, to the Lord Jesus Christ—the subject of Paul's letter and of my book—to whom I bow in magnificent surrender. Selah . . .

Foreword

A GROUP OF ICHTHYOLOGISTS recently undertook a daring experiment. They sought to genetically manipulate a certain species of fish to survive out of water. They succeeded beyond all expectation—not only could the fish breathe air, but it developed a phobia of water. The media gathered. This was a landmark event—a real scientific breakthrough.

A small stage was set up at the edge of a lake. The head scientist ascended the stage and welcomed the media. Then he reached into a black box and pulled out his fish. It looked exactly like its water-borne variety, except it breathed air. The reporters were suitably astonished. What drew their breath, though, was what happened next. The scientist held the fish over the lake. It flew into a panic, terrified at just the sight of wave slapping on wave. It twisted so hard that it broke free its grip and fell into the lake. Everyone watched in stunned silence. The fish at first lay deathly still. Then a quiver shot through its body. It fanned its gills, snapped its tail, and torpedoed away, gliding down through cool dark depths, in its element at last.

That's a made-up story.

But it's also a parable. God made us to live in him and for him. He "made us," to quote the apostle John, "to be a kingdom and priests to serve his God and Father" (Rev 1:6). When doing this or being this is when we're most fully alive. But the world has, for a long time, undertaken an experiment: it's sought to spiritually alter us to survive outside God's kingdom. Indeed, it's tried to breed in us an active fear of it. God's kingdom is our true home, but we've picked up a habit of resisting it.

And when, finally, we do fall in, most of us find we've survived so long outside his kingdom that we've lost all instinct for thriving in it. That's where Roger Helland meets us. Roger has thought long and studied hard on these matters. He has pondered deeply what it means to be fully alive in Christ and for Christ, and he's tested his insights in classrooms, in churches, with denominations, but mostly in his own life. In

Magnificent Surrender, he's distilled what he's learned into a field guide for kingdom living.

But Roger draws from an even deeper source. His book derives its force and depth from Paul's letter to the Colossians. Indeed, *Magnificent Surrender* is an extended pastoral reflection on and application of that letter. Colossians, in four brief chapters, presents the glory of Jesus Christ and the glory of a life wholly submitted to him. It is a manifesto of the rich life.

Magnificent Surrender heralds that brilliantly. It's a wise, loving and sometimes stern invitation to read Colossians again, with fresh eyes and fierce resolve. It's also a challenge to take to heart its promise and its exhortation—that we can and must, live in, through, with, and for Christ, who is all and in all, supreme and sufficient.

Well, enough of trying to sum it up. It's in your hands now. Take, and read. May it plunge you into the deep end, where at last you discover your true element.

Mark Buchanan
Author of *The Rest of God* and *Your Church is Too Safe*
www.markbuchanan.net

Preface

IF YOU WERE TO lead a Bible study, teach a course, or preach a series on revitalizing a church in the twenty-first century, how would you approach it? Would you use best-selling books, suggest successful models, and develop key practices? Would you, perhaps, point to the early church and the book of Acts? Would you explore the history of Christian renewal and revival movements as well as examples of growing churches, and then derive principles for revitalizing the church? What would be your assumptions? What would be your starting place?

I've experienced and written on church renewal, studied revivals and Acts, and read extensively on church growth, health, and revitalization. I've learned more than I can apply. When I enter church settings to coach them, my assumption is that most churches struggle with health; most Christians struggle with spiritual formation; and most models and principles are context-bound and unruly to export and reproduce elsewhere. I believe the axiom that "a church will never become what its leaders and people are not." Revitalized Christian people are what make revitalized churches. The starting place is *theological*, not structural or methodological. An institutional *temple spirituality* primarily oriented around church buildings, Sunday services, programs, formalized professional clergy, or standardized denominational frameworks, is not likely to produce a viral spiritual force of Christ followers and churches. Only a rigorous recovery of *Christology*—doctrine of Christ—will revitalize Christians. *He* must orient our lives.

The starting place, which still resumes for me, began in the fall of 2003 when I took a doctoral course with the late Dr. Stanley J. Grenz— "Revitalizing the Church in the Twenty-first Century." His assumption was that we all engage in life and ministry through our own *working theology*. I agree. We explored the role of theological reflection, which is a dynamic relationship between theology and ministry for effectiveness in Christ's service and the revitalization of the church in our postmodern world. He wrote, "Christians engage in theological reflection so that their lives might be changed. Theological reflection ought to foster godly spirituality and obedient discipleship. Indeed, good theology will make believers stronger, better informed, and consequently, more effective disciples. . . . Theology must be theocentric, *God centered*."[1]

We live what we believe. In the past fifteen years I've had my own theological paradigm revitalized concerning the nature and purpose of the church and what it means to be the people of God called to follow, obey, and surrender to the Lord Jesus Christ. I'm committed to the *missional church*—a group of incarnational Christ-followers who believe and behave as spiritual people for the sake of others, on mission together with Jesus Christ. *Missional church* is not just another church growth fad or just another church method to use. Rather, the *missional church* is a movement with a theological framework—a renewed trinitarian vision of the church as God's people who are commissioned as disciple-makers and *sent* as missionaries and witnesses, and as a royal priesthood into their communities, who embody and express the gospel in word and deed.

This became more acute when I taught a seminary course on the book of Colossians. I concluded that Paul's letter to the Colossians is a case study in theological reflection and contextualization for the purpose of church revitalization. Paul offers many *practices*—ways to behave—that flow from God-focused beliefs. He grounds church revitalization—spiritual formation, mission, and discipleship—in *Christology*. It's what I call a *missional spirituality*.

As you stroll through the priceless art gallery on display in the book of Colossians, my goal is to immerse you in theological reflection and invite you to adopt a posture of magnificent surrender to Christ Jesus as Lord. As you view his riches, may you discover that the central way to experience personal and corporate revitalization is to receive him *and* continue to live in him. We must hear Holy Scripture as God's living word addressed to us *today*. We must not settle for a mere study of what it meant to the church *then*. Theology is for today's church. Christian theology will instruct us in what to think and say about the trinitarian God, with the goal to know and love him more fully both as individuals and as entire congregations. Theology is transformational when we *apply* it. As you read my book along with a *theological* reading of Colossians, ponder the words of Lutheran Pietist New Testament scholar, Johann Albrecht Bengel (1687–1752), "Apply yourself wholly to the text; apply the text wholly to yourself."[2]

1. Grenz and Olson, *Who Needs Theology?*, 47.
2. Vanhoozer, *Dictionary for Theological Interpretation of the Bible*, 24.

Introduction: Jesus Is Lord

"As you have lived, so have you believed."[1]

How would you answer this question: What does it mean that *Jesus is Lord*? For seven months I met with a small group of pastors who gathered monthly to discuss how to develop a missional church. In our second meeting, the biblical assertion that *Jesus is Lord* was the heart of the discussion. We agreed that all the stunning colors of Christian theology, spirituality, and mission are refracted through a *Jesus is Lord* prism. But then I raised the question, "What does it mean in *your life* and in *your church* that Jesus is Lord?" A stone-faced silence stalled our discussion. You could embarrassingly tell that none of us had translated that abstract statement, which we all *believed*, into the concrete "days of our lives!" It took a few minutes for those three words, planted deeply into the soil of our imaginations, to emerge with a single blade of insight. One pastor remarked, "It means that Jesus is *sovereign* in our lives."

We made some progress, but then I asked: "Well then, what does it mean that Jesus is *sovereign*? If he really is sovereign, then what would that look like in how we live our lives and what would that look like in our churches?" In many ways, the entire New Testament unpacks the truth and its application to our daily lives that Jesus is *the* sovereign Lord and Savior. He's the eternal Creator-King and Sacrificial-Servant who rules and reigns in the Kingdom of God. As the Father's missionary, Jesus as Lord and Savior was the Sent One to seek and to save the lost and bring them home. He invites lost people to follow him, obey him, and serve him. As we discussed this theology we agreed that Jesus as sovereign also means that he's both *supreme* and *sufficient* for our lives and leadership. He's all we need. But it goes further—we must *ap-*

---

1. Søren Kierkegaard, as quoted by Vardy, *An Introduction to Kierkegaard*, 33.

ply this theology to the "days of our lives." We must learn to *surrender* and really *live* in the Lord.

LIVING IN THE LORD

Have you ever read or studied the book of Colossians? Over the years, I've read this short prison epistle of Paul and preached from some of its texts. But it wasn't until I prepared for a modular seminary course I was to teach on Colossians when I began to probe its vast riches like those contained in the oil sands of Alberta. Among many phrases we could offer from Colossians we cherish the often cited ones such as: "Christ, in whom are hidden all the treasures of wisdom and knowledge" (2:3), and: "For in Christ all the fullness of the Deity lives in bodily form" (2:9). But sandwiched between these statements about the sovereign Christ is the heart of the message of Colossians concerning our spiritual life in Christ: "So then, just as you received Christ Jesus as Lord, continue to live in him" (2:6). This verse serves as a hinge that turns the first section of the letter (Col 1:3–2:5) in the direction for all that follows in the second section (Col 2:7–4:6). This is the heart of Christian salvation and spirituality—centered in a magnificent surrender to Christ Jesus as Lord. Notice, we who *received* Christ Jesus as *Lord*, must continue to *live* in him.

The spiritual life is the surrendered life. Our view of Christ will shape our character and conduct. Someone said, "A religion never rises higher than its view of God." Colossians offers a towering view of Jesus Christ—one that is sublime, exalted, marked by stately grandeur and lavish beauty. Like a colossal magnifying glass, Colossians enlarges and glorifies Christ as the Lord beyond even the mind-boggling expanse of the universe itself. As seen in Luke 1:46–55, when Mary mused on her blessed fate to become the mother of Jesus, she launched into what's termed *The Magnificat* (Latin for *magnify*). She proclaimed, "My soul *magnifies* [glorifies] *the Lord!*" Earlier, after the angel Gabriel conveyed a confounding message to her about the virgin birth of Jesus, she replied, "I am the Lord's servant; may it be to me as you have said" (1:38). Mary practiced magnificent surrender. Paul's goal in Colossians is to compel us to do the same.

COLOSSIANS AND CHRIST

My book is a selected exploration, reflection, and application of Colossians—an invitation to the practice of magnificent surrender, which releases the riches of living in the Lord. In each chapter, we will drill into central texts that will uncover hidden treasure available to us as groups, churches, and individuals, when we *surrender* to Christ Jesus as *Lord*. His inexhaustible resources and his incomprehensible fullness are accessible to those who continue to live in him. Now remember, all theology is spiritual and practical not just intellectual. When we announce or argue against all other claims that *Jesus* is Lord, we trumpet a theological point and cement an absolute truth. Through the imperial cult, a Roman Caesar expected his subjects to worship and pay tribute to him. One of the titles attributed to Caesar was *kyrios* (Lord). But the early church refused to pledge allegiance to Caesar with their countercultural creed that *Jesus* is *kyrios*. If Jesus is Lord and we received him as such, we must obey, live in, and proclaim him. This was the issue in the Colossian church. Pagan culture, with its philosophies and spiritualities, dethroned Christ as Lord. Colossians 2 shows that not much has changed in two thousand years.

Colossae, a small rural town in the Lycus Valley in southwestern Turkey, sat in the shadow of two other important Roman cities with Christian churches—Laodicea (twelve miles west) and Hierapolis (fifteen miles northwest). Colossae, with a road that ran through it to Ephesus (120 miles west), trafficked in a potpourri of Oprah style philosophical and religious ideas that jeopardized the church there. The human traditions and teachings either diminished or discarded Jesus Christ as Lord. In the end, any claim to spirituality apart from or in addition to Christ is not Christian spirituality. When Paul wrote to counter the syncretism that had contaminated the church, Colossae was relatively insignificant. Soon after, an earthquake destroyed it. Nevertheless, Colossians contains some of the most significant Christian theology and spirituality in Scripture. Jammed into four short chapters (ninety-five verses), Colossians is a stunning art gallery of Christian theology, discipleship, spirituality, and mission. In it, Paul mentions the word *Christ* twenty-eight times! Like a giant *Imax* screen that enlarges a movie with enormous high definition detail, the book of Colossians enlarges Christ with enormous high definition detail as the sovereign, supreme, and sufficient Lord of all his creation and church.

MAGNIFICENT SURRENDER

In our third meeting together as pastors, we reviewed our previous discussion about Jesus as sovereign, about what the standards and practices were for fruitful discipleship, and how to cultivate a disciple-making church. We all agreed that disciple making must be the *heart*, not just a *part*, of church ministry.[2] At that point a pastor who had sat quiet remarked: "I've been a pastor in several churches for over twenty-five years. I've preached that Jesus is Lord, that we must fulfill the great commission to make disciples, and that simply doing church and going through the motions is not enough. But now I've been asking myself whether I'm surrendered to Jesus as sovereign in my life, and whether I'm a fully committed disciple myself." He lock jawed everyone's attention! As we shared what each of us planned to do in the next month before we re-gathered, this pastor announced: "I need to review my own life of discipleship and whether I'm going to do it, and ask what discipleship looks like and where Jesus is Lord in my life."

Then I remarked: "This has been a journey for me as well. I must go through a fearless spiritual inventory and let the Lord identify for me those areas that I must bring to him in a posture of surrender." Over the years I've sung the hymn *I Surrender All*, with the refrain, "I surrender all, I surrender all, all to thee, my blessed Savior, I surrender all." Perhaps you have too. I remember many times where I felt a slight twinge in my heart because I knew the heresy of my life did not match the orthodoxy of the hymn. I've thought, "Do I—do we—really surrender all?" Come on! Look around us. Do we? Do I? If so, then why do I have control issues, why do I get rattled about money, and why do I become anxious when faced with complex decisions? Why don't I surrender all areas of my life that I continue to clench onto, like a baby who says "mine!" and won't let go of a toy? I review my life and see that God has consistently answered prayer, blessed me, and provided for my wife and me. I know Jesus said, "Fear not." And yet, I can be as anxious and obnoxious as a fearful back seat driver. The issue comes down to *trust*.

In 2007 I completed my doctorate, was unemployed, and had a restless passion to return to full-time teaching in a seminary or Bible college. I had applied to a prominent seminary in eastern Canada, was flown in

2. A point well developed by Bill Hull in *The Disciple-making Pastor*. For specific disciple-making habits and practices see, Alan Hirsch with Darryn Altclass, *The Forgotten Ways Handbook: A Practical Guide for Missional Churches*, 63–85.

for two days of interviews, and returned home with the assumption that I landed the position. Not! That threw me for a huge loop because I had no job and no direction, and my daughter was to marry that summer. In a matter of three God-seeking months, I came into a denominational position in Alberta, gave away our daughter in marriage, moved from a community and province we had lived in for over twenty years, and basically started over as an empty nester. We left behind our two sons, our friends, our church, our home, and our ministry in the lives of countless people, to follow Jesus on an uncertain venture—which produced *angst*. Many times along the way I took matters into my hands to "get it done"!

Now, five years later, I look back and again marvel how God led in subversive and meticulous ways. A move to eastern Canada might have been unfruitful and lonely. It was very far away, untimely, and limiting; even though I obsessed over it and was angry with God because I thought that's where we were to go. Our daughter and husband and second son moved here. Many teaching and writing opportunities opened up here. Our new jobs have been excellent here. And God prepared in advance numerous ministry outlets into the lives of people in our new life here. Aren't we all in the same boat? I imagine if we all lived more surrendered lives to our sovereign Lord we would lead more missional lives. We'd not fear. We'd be courageous. We'd be focused and not distracted by things that don't ultimately matter. We'd *trust*.

Why do many of us we miss this? Is it because, at the core, we don't *trust* Jesus? Is it because we are trapped in control and consumption? Do we merely consign Jesus to our lives like a guest to our spare bedroom rather than live with him and he live with us in our whole house (John 15)? Is Jesus only the part-time Lord of our religious life and not the full-time Lord of our whole life? Perhaps the issue for us, as it was for the Colossians, is a *theological* one, which requires that we re-imagine, re-orient, and repent our way back into spiritual formation and discipleship. Eugene Peterson offers a challenge:

> If Christ is King, everything, quite literally, every *thing* and every *one*, has to be re-imagined, re-configured, re-oriented to a way of life that consists in an obedient following of Jesus. This is not easy. It is not accomplished by participating in a prayer meeting or two, or signing up for a seven-step course in discipleship

at school or church, or attending an annual prayer breakfast. A total renovation of our imagination, our way of looking at things—what Jesus commanded in his no-nonsense imperative, "Repent!"—is required.[3]

For faith and obedience we need a Mount Everest view of the person and work of the Lord Jesus Christ that will tower above all else. From that vantage point the panorama is breathtaking. When the truth of who Christ really is settles into our theological imaginations, like the team that scales the summit of Everest, we will want to absorb the grandeur and glory of the view and stay up there a very long time. That way when we settle back into the valley and into the routines of daily life, we are forever changed as our gaze constantly returns to that summit. For growth in Christian spirituality we do not need more of church but more of Christ. In fact, Paul declares, "The glorious riches of this mystery is Christ in you, the hope of glory" (1:27).

Open your New Testament to the book of Colossians. Follow along as we explore what a life of magnificent surrender looks like. My prayer is that when we finish this exploration together, you'll be able to aptly answer the question, "What does it mean that Jesus is Lord?"

REFLECTION FOR GROUPS AND INDIVIDUALS

1. When you read, *Jesus is Lord*, what comes to mind? What does this mean for your group, church, and individual life?

2. When you read, *the spiritual life is the surrendered life*, what comes to mind? What does this mean? What images emerge when you reflect on the words, *magnificent surrender*? How would you practice this in your group, church, and individual life?

3. When you read about the pastor who after twenty-five years now questions what it means to be a disciple and have Jesus as Lord of his life, if you are a pastoral leader, what do you think of your own life and leadership?

PRACTICE FOR GROUPS AND INDIVIDUALS

1. Reflect on Kierkegaard's quote, "*As you have lived, so have you believed.*" How might you trace your behavior back to your beliefs,

3. Peterson, *The Jesus Way*, 8–9.

as a group, as a church, and as an individual? Do a spiritual inventory. What does your evaluation reveal, both positive and negative? Develop three practices for future growth.

2. With open hands, daily pray the prayer of relinquishment. Pray: "May your will be done in my life as it is in heaven" (Matt 6:10), and: "I am the Lord's servant, may it be to me as you say" (Luke 1:38). Read the following quote as a group or individual regularly:

   "The Spirit teaches me to yield my will entirely to the will of the Father. He opens my ear to wait in great gentleness and teachableness of soul for what the Father has day by day to speak and to teach. He discovers to me how union with God's will is union with God Himself; how entire surrender to God's will is the Father's claim, the Son's example, and the true blessedness of the soul."
   —Andrew Murray

3. Memorize Colossians 1:27, "The glorious riches of this mystery is Christ in you, the hope of glory." Study this text in several translations and consult several commentaries to unlock its meaning and practical significance. How can you apply this text to your group, church, and individual life?

1

Faith and Fruit

*"Yes, I am the vine; you are the branches. Those who remain
in me, and I in them, will produce much fruit. For apart from
me you can do nothing." (John 15:5, NLT)*

I LIVED IN KELOWNA with my wife and our three children for twenty-two glorious years. A thriving city of 110,000, Kelowna sits gracefully like a solitaire diamond on beautiful Lake Okanagan in the British Columbia interior, four hours east of Vancouver. The lake is home to the legendary Loch Ness-type creature called Ogopogo. Kelowna is a picturesque life giving "staycation," tourist, and retirement hub with moderate climate and multiple outdoor activities. In 1859 a Catholic priest named Father Pandosy and a small group of oblates established the first settlement of white people there—now known as Father Pandosy's Mission—southeast of downtown Kelowna. They offered healing and hope to the area's Indian and growing settler populations. As a former mission outpost, Kelowna now radiates two redemptive features: 1) *faith*—it's home to many strong churches and Christian-led businesses like the Society of Hope (which develops low cost housing), and Club Penguin (a children's interactive website); and 2) *fruit*—it's home to numerous wineries, orchards, and the Sun-Rype fruit juice manufacturing company. What you see in the spiritual (*faith*) is what you see in the natural (*fruit*).

Our family enjoyed some of the most succulent peaches, cherries, and apples in the world. Kelowna and the entire Okanagan Valley produce world-class fruitfulness. *God is into fruit.* The opening chapters of Genesis show God's design for the fruitfulness of both creation and the human race. He crafted the Garden of Eden and the tree of life to offer good and pleasing fruit for Adam and Eve. He also commanded the first

1

couple to be fruitful and multiply. In the Old Testament, God considered Israel his vineyard and he expected fruitfulness from his people. In the same way, Jesus uses the vine and branches metaphor to depict the vital union between he and his followers where he expects and empowers much fruit in them (John 15:1–17).

What is the one practice, which you must cultivate and use to bear succulent spiritual fruit in your life in the Lord? Pray? Worship? Read Scripture? Serve God? Attend church? Nope. There's something more difficult and formidable. Without it, you can't bear spiritual fruit. It's *faith*. We know that "without faith it's impossible to please God" (Heb 11:6). For some, faith is a word about *optimism*: "Just have faith!" In Scripture, faith is a word about *confidence*. Observe Colossians 1:3–6. Note the vital connection between faith and fruit:

> We always thank God, the Father of our Lord Jesus Christ, when we pray for you, because we have heard of your *faith* in Christ Jesus and of the love you have for all the saints—the *faith* and love that spring from the hope that is stored up for you in heaven and that you have already heard about in the word of truth, the gospel that has come to you. All over the world this gospel is bearing *fruit* and growing, just as it has been doing among you since the day you heard it and understood God's grace in all its truth.

THEOLOGICAL VIRTUES

Like the wardrobe that transported four children into the enchanted world of Narnia where "Aslan is on the move," faith transports us all into the enchanted world of God's kingdom where the "gospel is on the move." This gospel, received by faith in Christ Jesus, comes to people *among* people, as it bears fruit and grows all over the world. Since its inception, Christianity has been the most aggressive spiritual movement on earth. The Gospel trumpets the word of truth—saturated with grace—which we always need to hear. Even as inspiration can come through hearing our favorite artist on the radio, we must continue to believe that faith comes through hearing the word of God (Rom 10:17). As we *hear* God's word, it sustains our faith. A.W. Tozer reminds us, "Faith comes first to the hearing ear, not to the cogitating mind."[1]

---

1. A. W. Tozer, as cited by Wiersbe, *The Bible Exposition Commentary*, Luke 8:4–15.

Christian faith isn't a *stationary* set of doctrines or creeds that we merely affirm intellectually. Rather, it's a *dynamic* trust in the person of Jesus Christ. Recently, I read Peter Vardy's *An Introduction to Kierkegaard*. Kierkegaard views faith as *existential*. He posits that a person must continuously choose to stake their life on a truth claim about Jesus Christ (God in flesh) that reason might otherwise reject. This requires that we choose and think in a dynamic rather than in a static way. It is subjective and not purely intellectual or objective. To illustrate it, Vardy mentions a scene from the movie *Indiana Jones and the Last Crusade* (1989). He writes:

> Jones is seeking the Holy Grail—the cup from which Jesus is supposed to have drunk wine at the Last Supper. Nazis who are also seeking the Grail capture him and his father is seriously injured. The only hope of saving his father is to find the Grail. Indiana Jones evaded the Nazis and raced down an underground cavern at the end of which, a secret map has told him where the Grail is located. He comes to a halt before a huge precipice of immeasurable depth. On the other side of this chasm is the Holy Grail. The map tells him that if he steps out over the chasm a hidden bridge will appear. He cannot test whether the bridge is there or not—he has to stake his whole life on his belief that the bridge exists though there is no guarantee that it does. Jones is required to have faith that the bridge exists. This is not simply intellectual faith. He has to stake his life on the existence of the bridge by putting all his weight on it. If the bridge does not appear he will fall to the bottom of the chasm and die. In a similar way, for Kierkegaard, faith requires individuals to stake their lives on a claim (the incarnation) that may or may not be true. Faith, therefore, is an existential act.[2]

When Scottish missionary John G. Paton translated Scripture into the language of the Gaelic tribes in the New Hebrides islands, he searched for an exact word to translate *faith*. After a diligent search, he discovered the right word. It meant: "lean your whole weight upon." Living in the Lord does not mean: "Just have faith," or "I hope things work out." To have biblical faith is to place your trust in Christ Jesus. To place your trust in Christ Jesus, as Lord, is to believe him as you lean your whole life upon him as you would lean against a wall. It's to acknowledge him as sovereign in your heart, not as an abstract doctrine in your head.

2. Vardy, *An Introduction to Kierkegaard*, 24–25.

Faith includes *surrender*. Paul Little wrote two well-known books, *Know What You Believe* and *Know Why You Believe*. Recently, his wife collected and edited his writings to compile a final book entitled, *Know Who You Believe*. When we know *who* we believe, his sovereign love charms our hearts into magnificent surrender. Who is Jesus Christ? Is he the Lord and Savior on whom we lean our faith practically, or is he a doctrine or a theological subject we believe and study intellectually?

Righteous people live by faith (Rom 1:17), not sight (2 Cor 5:7). This is a one-time decision to trust Christ as Savior for forgiveness and eternal life because he's trustworthy as *Messiah*. It's also a repeated decision to trust Christ for guidance and destiny in life because he's trustworthy as *Lord*. The *New Living Translation* puts it this way, "It is through faith that a righteous person has life." It's with assurance and actions of hopeful trust that a person in right relationship to God shall live and have life. Have a careful read of Hebrews 11—the "hall of faith"—that offers a compelling survey of ancients whom God commends. The key repeated phrase in this chapter is, *by faith* . . . You'll notice what each ancient did *by faith*. By faith Abel offered a better sacrifice than Cain; by faith Noah built an ark; by faith Abraham obeyed and went to a place in which he did not know where he was going; by faith the people passed through the Red Sea; by faith Rahab the prostitute welcomed the spies—all commended for their faith.

I don't know about you, but I find it hard to live by faith. I'm a task-oriented person who likes to make things happen and see results. I grew up with the humanistic philosophy that "you can accomplish whatever you set your mind to" and "God helps those who help themselves." I've since learned this is bad theology. But, sometimes it feels like God isn't doing anything. I have to make an important decision. So, I pray, I wait on God, I talk to my wife, I try to "hear God's voice," I think, and then . . . nothing . . . more questions and anxiety. Like a restless child in the back seat whining: "Are we there yet?" I can feel impatient and faithless.

And then I read, "The apostles said to the Lord, 'Increase our faith!' Jesus replied, 'If you have faith as small as a mustard seed, you can say to this mulberry tree, 'Be uprooted and planted in the sea,' and it will obey you'" (Luke 17:5–6). OK, so all I need is mustard seed-sized faith to move deep-rooted situations in my life. I'm encouraged because the apostles also needed a faith increase. They couldn't see how to forgive someone seven times a day. For years I refused to forgive my father just once. While I was a PhD student in Montréal at McGill University, my wife helped me with that! But I'm also discouraged because I have a real mustard seed in a little baggie on a bookshelf in my home office, to remind me to increase my faith. It doesn't! It's tiny, and I can't seem to trust Christ, even in tiny ways? Someone said, "If you think it takes size to be effective you've never been to bed with a mosquito!" The kingdom of God works like a tiny mustard seed. Hudson Taylor labeled faith as the "exchanged life." He mused, "But how to get faith strengthened? Not by striving after faith, but by resting on the Faithful One."[3]

When we rest our faith on the immovable Rock of Gibraltar Christ as Lord, the century-long curse of perpetual winter cast by the evil white witch over our own personal Narnia is broken. We can then serve as members of God's royal priesthood as kings and queens, where faith leads a threesome of theological virtues called faith, love, and hope. These become the charter for kingdom living in the Lord. Paul and Timothy thanked God when they prayed for the Colossians because they had heard that faith, love, and hope were active and growing among them as a church. Paul also showcased these theological virtues in his letters to the Corinthians (1 Cor 13:13) and to the Thessalonians (1 Thess 1:3).

Paul heard of the *faith* the Colossians had in Christ but also of the *love* they had for all the saints (1:4). He also noted this virtue about the Ephesians (Eph 1:15) and Philemon (Phlm 5). Faith, love, and hope are theological virtues, as they find their source and substance in God— foundations for our moral life of virtue. When Christians love one another, they prove that they are disciples of Jesus (John 13:35). What would it mean to love all the believers in your church, even difficult people? What would it mean to love your neighbor as yourself? Jon Stewart remarked, "Remember to love your neighbor as you love yourself. And if you hate yourself, then please—just leave your neighbor alone!"[4] What if Christians loved others the way God intended?

Friends of ours, Daniel and Laurie, pastor at Mountain Springs Church in Colorado Springs. Burdened by God's love for others, they, along with the other pastors and leaders, helped launch a church-wide mission to their local community called *Impact: Revolution of Love*. It is part of their overall vision for the church to "live the mission" of Jesus by serving others in tangible ways. They cancel the weekend worship

3. Taylor, *Hudson Taylor's Spiritual Secret*, 76.

4. Jon Stewart, quoted by David Dark, *The Sacredness of Questioning Everything*, 9.

services a couple of times per year. The entire weekend becomes worship through service in the community where people sign up and are sent out on organized missions to help and love needy people in practical ways.

Donna Lowe, whom I know from a church where I pastored in Kelowna, wrote *Radical Love*. She posted this on *Facebook*: "When God's love radically changes us, we become empowered to love others. It starts with our hearts, and then proves God's existence to others. Alone, you will have an effect. Imagine, however, if we all joined together in one heart and one mind to bear witness to the world that God's love (like no other love), will forever change them."

In our book *Missional Spirituality: Embodying God's Love From the Inside Out*, Len Hjalmarson and I unpack the meaning and offer practices in how we can love our Lord God from all our heart, soul, mind, and strength, and our neighbor as our self. It starts with our hearts. We define missional spirituality as: "*an attentive and active engagement of embodied love for God and neighbor expressed from the inside out.*"[5] Christian spirituality is *relational*. When we live by the Spirit we are spiritual. To grow spiritually we must grow relationally in our love for others. Paul teaches, "The *only* thing that counts is *faith* expressing itself through *love*" (Gal 5:6). Is this the only thing that counts? Pietist theologian Johann Arndt wrote, "If faith shares with a neighbor the blessings that it has itself received, love arises out of faith, and imparts to the neighbor that which it has itself received from God."[6]

I'm married to a deeply spiritual woman whose integrity is impeccable. My wife Gail loves deeply. She always puts the interests of others (especially her children and me) above her own. She is generous, willing to forgive, thoughtful, and eager to help people. Her virtue continuously warms and blesses those around her. She rarely offends, always listens, and receives compliments from family, friends, and those at her workplace. She teaches me how to love and be relational. It's no surprise that she also models rock solid faith and hope.

Paul continues, "We have heard of your faith in Christ Jesus and of the love you have for all the saints, the faith and love that spring from the *hope* that is stored up for you in heaven and that you have already heard about in the word of truth, the gospel that has come to you" (1:4–5). Like an Olympic gymnast catapulted by a springboard, when we hear about

---

5. Helland and Hjalmarson, *Missional Spirituality*, 31.

6. Arndt, *True Christianity*, 23.

stored up hope in heaven, it catapults our faith and love into action. This is why the gospel is good news. When people hear about *the* hope chest stored in heaven, it banishes fear of death and inspires one to live by faith and love rather than by sight and selfishness. This isn't the "I hope so" brand of mere wishful thinking. Rather, it's an eternal perspective based on the person of Jesus Christ, our hope. Like superglue, faith clings to hope. Someone said, "Hope is the ability to hear the music of the future; faith is the courage to dance to it today."

We all need hope to face life and death. I grew up in Southern California where I knew of the City of Hope in the nearby town of Duarte, northeast of Los Angeles. It's a one hundred-acre park-like cancer treatment and research center. Their website says, "For many people, City of Hope is where hope begins" and "Compassion drives our innovation." It's interesting how hope for a cancer cure drives their compassion for patients. As I have had prostate cancer myself, I understand how both hope and compassion work together. In this life, the gospel is the only hope for a cure regarding sin and death as our hope is secured for the life to come. Bill Hybels often proclaims, "The church is the hope of the world." But the New Testament doesn't technically proclaim this. It proclaims that Jesus Christ and the gospel are the hope of the world.

Paul wrote that this gospel, like a Costco warehouse jam-packed with goods stored from floor to ceiling, carries a message of stored up hope in heaven itself. We don't come to this gospel. Like the news posted daily to our email or home page, this gospel *comes to us* (1:6)! The good news of hope in Jesus Christ is a personified *movement*. How does faith travel? It's active and on the move *through people*. Hirsch and Ferguson write, "Christianity is designed to be a people's liberation movement, a social force, a viral idea passing from person to person through the medium of gospel and discipleship, creating gospel communities in its wake."[7]

This hope is a powerful incentive to love others in the community of faith—all the saints (1:4). Because our own future is secure in heaven, and because we place our faith in Christ, we are free to look after the needs of others. It requires faith to love others because when we love, we look not to our own interests but to the interests of others (Phil 2:4). We see the theological virtues in action: *faith* expressed through *love* springs from the *hope* stored up for us in heaven. Notice the communal nature of

7. Hirsch and Ferguson, *On the Verge*, 32.

spirituality: "Be devoted to *one another* in brotherly *love*. Honor *one another* above yourselves. Never be lacking in zeal, but *keep your spiritual fervor*, serving the Lord. Be joyful in *hope*, patient in affliction, faithful in prayer" (Rom 12:10–12).

Is it possible that a church, which lacks love, is also one, which lacks hope, and even faith? As a denominational leader, I work with many churches that have problems. Some problems are about philosophies of ministry, some are about styles of worship or leadership, but often, the problems are about relationships that lack Christian love and faith. I see how fear can drain the life out of a church. Every dollar is an issue; every decision is an ordeal; every perspective is a criticism. Often church leaders ask: "How do we grow our church"? Many are concerned with so-called "church growth" and "church health," and seek to apply technology rather than spirituality for results—try this program, cast this vision, and attract more people.

Christian leaders will use various standards to measure the success of their churches such as an increase in attendance, baptisms, offerings, and programs, or the quality of preaching, worship, and leadership. Whether the setting is a small church trying to stay alive or a large church trying to grow larger, lots of time, energy, and money is spent on facilities and bottom lines, while the imagination for ministry is held hostage. Is it possible to succeed in all these areas and still lack health or maturity? Is it possible to develop a mature church without an increase in faith, love, and hope? Can we measure these?

Apparently we can, as both the Colossians and Thessalonians had reputations for these virtues and the Corinthians did not. What would happen if we focused on strategies that would help us increase in faith, hope, and love, and focused on ways to measure these as our benchmarks of Christian spirituality? With the Thessalonians, Paul must have applied some specific metrics to remember before God their "work produced by faith, labor prompted by love, and endurance inspired by hope" (1 Thess 1:3). In fact the Lord's message "rang out" like a cathedral bell from their entire region and their faith in God had become known everywhere (1:9). They had a reverberating reputation of faith and hope as they "turned to God from idols to serve the living and true God and to wait for his Son from heaven" (1:9). To live in the Lord, we must embody these theological virtues, and then we will bear much spiritual fruit.

While church leaders tend to focus on church *management*, what about Christian *mission*? What about a group of revolutionaries who, through radical love, seek and save the lost? Isn't the church to be a movement of missionary people who embody Jesus in deed and word in their networks, neighborhoods, and workplaces? Churches often have an inward focus without any outward focus. In Canada, for a church to get a tax number and hold charitable status as a non-profit society, it must demonstrate that it offers a direct benefit to its community. If not, it ceases to be a missional church and becomes a social club. One church is involved in a ministry called *Work of Your Hand*. It helps disadvantaged artisans who up-cycle juice packs and coffee sacks into colorful bags, purses, wallets, potholders, oven mitts, and aprons. At Christmas, members purchase their colorful large shopping bags at fair wage prices, fill them with non-perishable food items, and give them to needy people. This ministry simultaneously assists poor artisans in the Philippines and hungry single parents and street people in Calgary. Creative love!

FRUIT BEARING

I grew up in Southern California near Orange County—home of Disneyland, Knott's Berry Farm, and forty miles of sun-baked beaches. Until urban expansion, Southern California was largely a vast patchwork of luscious fruit trees cultivated in orchards or groves: orange, lemon, grapefruit, peach, apricot, walnut, and avocado. As a boy I played in many orchards and picked these fruits from their trees to revel in mouth-dazzling fruit. There was so much it was overwhelming. You now know how Orange County and Garden Grove got their names. Garden Grove offers the highest number of churches and places of worship per capita in California. Orange County, affluent and ambitious, produced renowned Christian leaders such as Charles Swindoll, Chuck Smith, John Wimber, and Rick Warren. It's an orchard full of faith and fruit.

So was Colossae. The gospel that bore fruit and grew all over the world also flourished among the Colossian believers (Col 1:6). The gospel isn't an impersonal religious item advertized on billboards or archived in theology textbooks. It's a living message unleashed by God's power in the resurrected Jesus Christ who is active in the world as *Lord*. This gospel bears fruit and grows when we embody it with our lives and express it with our lips. It's what Hugh Halter calls "the tangible kingdom" and what I call "the gospel according to you." God programmed fruit bearing into the DNA of creation itself. Nature and the human race itself cannot survive without fruitfulness. From the seeds of trees sown in receptive soil, to the seeds of males sown in receptive wombs, to the seeds of the Word sown in receptive hearts, God's *telos* (goal) is fruit bearing. Living *in* the Lord will release the riches of much fruit, made possible only when we're in spiritual union with Christ. Here's an interpretation of his words:

> Live in me. Make your home in me just as I do in you. In the same way that a branch can't bear grapes by itself but only by being joined to the vine, you can't bear fruit unless you are joined with me. I am the Vine, you are the branches. When you're joined with me and I with you, the relation intimate and organic, the harvest is sure to be abundant. Separated, you can't produce a thing. . . . This is how my Father shows who he is—when you produce grapes, when you mature as my disciples. I've loved you the way my Father has loved me. Make yourselves at home in my love. If you keep my commands, you'll remain intimately at home in my love. That's what I've done—kept my Father's commands and made myself at home in his love. (John 15:4–10, *The Message*)

The key to fruitfulness is living in the Lord—an organic union where we make our home in him. There are two vital practices to sustain this homemaking: 1) obey Christ's words, and 2) remain in Christ's love. The nutrients that feed this union are Christ's infinite love for us—the same infinite love that he has from the Father. This is radical, magnificent love and surrender! Is it true that Jesus loves us the way his Father loves him? Like a parent who loves each child the same, Jesus loves us the same as the Father loves him. But that's not all; he also keeps his Father's commands. This pathway of surrender results in fruit. Jesus also taught, "Make a tree good and its fruit will be good, or make a tree bad and its fruit will be bad, for a tree is recognized by its fruit" (Matt 12:33). Like a stunning nine-pearled necklace that adorns a royal princess, the nine-fold fruit of the Spirit should adorn all believers as royal priests: love, joy, peace, patience, kindness, goodness, faithfulness, gentleness, and self-control" (Gal 5:22–23).

Paul continues: "We have not stopped praying for you and asking God to fill you with the knowledge of his will through all spiritual wisdom and understanding. And we pray this in order that you may *live a life worthy of the Lord* and may *please him* in every way: *bearing fruit* in every good work, *growing* in the knowledge of God" (1:9–10). Living in the Lord means we live in a way that honors and pleases him, as we bear fruit and increasingly get to know God. Like compounding interest, we'll grow exponentially as we advance from knowing God's will to knowing God himself.

I preached a sermon on Ephesians 5:1–2, 8–10. My theme was: "Be Something." I spoke to a church in Calgary that had studied Miles McPherson's book *Do Something*. This church had shifted to an outward focus and sought to do something and serve their community for Christ. I encouraged them that as they *do* something they must also *be* something, namely—"*Be* imitators of God and live a life of love and light" in their community.

On our way home my wife mused with me on verses 8–10, "For you were once darkness, but now you are light in the Lord. Live as children of light . . . and find out what pleases the Lord." She wondered what the connection was between live as children of light and find out what pleases the Lord. That's a great question. We must insure that we walk in the light where all goodness, righteousness, and truth will become evident in our character and conduct (Eph 5:9). On the other hand, we must insure that we live in such way that we consider what pleases the Lord. She also recalled the time when as a new Christian she read that last part for the first time, "And find out what pleases the Lord." She had wondered: "How do I find out what pleases the Lord? I want to please him with my life." Because the spiritual life is a surrendered life, the Lord's agenda becomes ours. Imagine the Lord not being pleased with you! Some of us are people-pleasers bound by the opinions and expectations of others. Let's be God-pleasers.

Paul prayed that the Colossians would "please him in every way, bear fruit in every good work, and grow in the knowledge of God." This is living in the Lord—Christian spirituality at its core. How do we accomplish this? Go back to verse 9: "Ask God to fill you with the knowledge of his will through all spiritual wisdom and understanding." Like the house filled with the fragrance of the perfumed ointment Mary poured on Jesus' feet (John 12:3), may your life be filled with the fragrance of his will through the wisdom and understanding the Holy Spirit gives.

I love the word *fragrance* and its image for the aroma of piety, love, and Jesus. Picture yourself as a Mary—bent down before Jesus—humble, imperfect, and devout. You pour your life out on him—costly, broken, and received. Paul says you are God's fragrance: "But thanks be to God, who always leads us in triumphal procession in Christ and through us spreads everywhere the *fragrance* of the knowledge of him. For we are to God the aroma of Christ among those who are being saved and those who are perishing" (2 Cor 2:14–15). Like *Chanel No. 5*, you are an expensive fragrance and aroma of Christ wherever you are in your world.

The faith and fruit in the Colossian church did not emerge from abstract ideas. They emerged from Epaphras, a local Colossian resident. Paul called him a dear fellow servant (slave) and faithful minister (deacon) (Col 1:7). Epaphras, who likely heard Paul during his three-year stay in Ephesus, became a convert who returned to his hometown as a local missionary. Later, when Paul wrote from prison to Philemon—another local from Colossae—he sent greetings from Epaphras his fellow prisoner (Phlm 23). Paul also sent Epaphras' greetings to the Colossians, whom he identifies as one of them, and a servant (slave) of Christ Jesus (Col 4:12). Epaphras always wrestled (agonized) in prayer for the Colossians, that they would "stand firm in all the will of God, *mature* and fully assured" (Col 4:12). As a modern-day Epaphras, never underestimate your potential to help disciple others toward maturity, through your faithful service and tireless prayer. As a slave of Christ Jesus, you can be a gospel messenger in your own community. It all starts and continues, like Ignatius of Loyola, with magnificent surrender.

Ignatius (1491–1556) was a Spanish knight who became a Catholic Church reformer and founder of the *Society of Jesus* (Jesuits). After a leg injury inflicted by a cannon ball, he recuperated at the castle in Loyola, Spain where he read Ludolph of Saxony's book on contemplative prayer entitled *Life of Christ*. Inspired to become a soldier for Christ, Ignatius would make lifelong vows of poverty, chastity, and obedience, as he consecrated himself irrevocably to God. In 1534 he and six companions founded the *Society of Jesus*. This society ventured into the community to teach, preach, help others, and spread the faith. Ignatius also placed a high value on academic preparation for ministry. By the time of his death, the order had grown to over one thousand Jesuits with a network of seventy-four colleges on three continents. Perhaps you'd like to pray his prayer of surrender:

> Take, O Lord, and receive my entire liberty, my memory, my understanding and my whole will. All that I am and all that I possess you have given me. I surrender it all to you to be disposed of according to your will. Give me only your love and your grace; with these I will be rich enough, and will desire nothing more.

REFLECTION FOR GROUPS AND INDIVIDUALS

1. How would you describe *faith*? Why is it the key to a righteous life and fruitfulness? Read through Hebrews 11. How is faith described and depicted there? How can you as a group, church, or individual increase in faith and measure it?

2. How would you describe *love*? How is it that the only thing that counts is faith expressing itself through love (Gal 5:6)? Observe and reflect on John 15:1–17. How does love cultivate fruitfulness in our union with Christ and validate our discipleship? How can you as a group, church, or individual increase in love and measure it?

3. How would you describe *hope*? How is hope a springboard for faith and love? What does the image of hope stored up in heaven communicate to you? Describe or reflect on situations where people need a future hope that can assist them in present circumstances. How can you as a group, church, or individual increase in hope and measure it?

PRACTICE FOR GROUPS AND INDIVIDUALS

1. Use faith, hope, and love as a structure and substance for spiritual growth in your group, church, and individual life. Do a concordance study of these words in the New Testament. Find ways for faith to express itself in love as you are reminded of the hope stored up for you in heaven.

2. Practice *union with Christ* each day as you seek to make your home in him, through obedience to his commands and loving people. Read a good commentary on John 15:1–17.

3. Like Epaphras, regularly wrestle in prayer for your group and church to "stand firm in all the will of God, *mature* and fully assured" and seek ways to be a missionary in your community.

2

He Is . . .

"I have one passion—it is He, it is He alone."[1]

I GREW UP IN a non-Christian family where "Jesus Christ" was a swear word and "God damn it" was a frustration mantra. Our family never once attended a church service. We knew no Christians though we knew some people who were "religious"—like the polite Japanese teenager next door who babysat me when I was little. However, I do remember one occasion, when I was about six, where my mother asked if I wanted to try out Sunday school. My first thought was, "School on *Sunday*?" As a young lad, those words sounded about as exciting as "eat your vegetables because they are good for you!" But I tried it, in what I think was an old Presbyterian church. My mother escorted me down creaking stairs to a dingy basement to sit on hard wooden pews with about five other kids. Then she left. The stiff, hair-bunned teacher with her blackboard and lesson, made a stale impression on me that Jesus was boring and lived a long time ago. I never returned. I don't blame my parents or the old-fashioned Sunday school teacher. Like the thirty-three Chilean miners trapped in a dark mine for over two months, I was trapped in the dominion of darkness from which God would rescue me (Col 1:13). A dozen years later through my first act of faith, he brought me into the kingdom of the Son he loves (Col 1:13).

People ask me, "When you were growing up, what was your background?" My reply: "Pagan!" I was darkness—a lightless cavern of seething sin. Like some of your stories, my story parallels some of the Corinthians:

1. Moravian leader, Count Nicholas Ludwig von Zinzendorf, quoted by Kirby Page, *Living Abundantly*, 322.

Do not be deceived: Neither the sexually immoral nor idolaters nor adulterers nor male prostitutes nor homosexual offenders nor thieves nor the greedy nor drunkards nor slanderers nor swindlers will inherit the kingdom of God. *And that is what some of you were.* But you were washed, you were sanctified, you were justified in the name of the Lord Jesus Christ and by the Spirit of our God." (1 Cor 6:9–11)

The last two propositions record my spiritual history: "And that is what some of you *were. But* you were *washed*, you were *sanctified*, you were *justified* in the name of the Lord Jesus Christ and by the Spirit of our God"! I was certainly much of what some of the Corinthians *were.* That word *but* is small in size, though enormous in significance—*but* you were washed, sanctified, and justified in the Lord Jesus Christ. These colossal theological realities script many of our journeys from darkness to light, death to life, sin to salvation, ruin to redemption! In December 1969, I was home on Christmas leave from boot camp while in the U.S. Army at Fort Ord, California. One Friday night, Danny, a high school friend, and I went up on Glendora Mountain Road to overlook the city where as teens we would all go to drink and smoke dope. While I was at Fort Ord, Danny became a "Jesus freak." That Friday night while I peaked on LSD he told me about Jesus! I prayed my first prayer ever, that if Jesus was real I wanted to believe. That winter night *the gospel came to me* through Danny, my local missionary.

Paul's interest in the Corinthians and in the Colossians, in an eighteen year-old doper, and in you, is theological and spiritual. Christian spirituality is the *practice* of applied Christian theology. All theology must be practical. Dr. Harold Hoehner of Dallas Seminary taught, "*We can no longer live as we once did because we are no longer the people we once were.*" Christ is not a Sunday school flannel graph character but the supreme Lord of the universe who can reach a lost teenager stoned on acid through another former doper sent on a mission. From then on, even as the Colossians needed to know *who* Jesus was, so do we. Living in the Lord requires knowledge of the Lord. Christian spirituality begins with a magnificent surrender to Jesus Christ who is . . .

THE BEGINNING

The ultimate theological question of all time is, "Who is Jesus Christ?" What we believe about the Lord Jesus Christ, according to Scripture, sets the framework for both our salvation and our spirituality (sanctification). That's why Paul very early in his letter to the Colossians hustles like an NFL running back straight for the theological identity of Christ. As we shall see in Colossians 2, like many postmodern people today, the Colossians fell into spiritual syncretism because they lacked a supreme and sufficient theological view of the Creator-Redeemer Christ. So, let's explore how to apply Christian theology for Christian spirituality.

An effective method for Bible study is to engage the text according to this pattern: 1) observation, 2) interpretation, and 3) application. The more time you spend observing key terms, structure, and grammar will offer more insights for interpretation and application. How might your theology affect your spirituality? Observe Colossians 1:15–20:

> He is the image of the invisible God, the firstborn over all creation. For by him all things were created: things in heaven and on earth, visible and invisible, whether thrones or powers or rulers or authorities; all things were created by him and for him. He is before all things, and in him all things hold together. And he is the head of the body, the church; he is the beginning and the firstborn from among the dead, so that in everything he might have the supremacy. For God was pleased to have all his fullness dwell in him, and through him to reconcile to himself all things, whether things on earth or things in heaven, by making peace through his blood, shed on the cross.

This passage, a sung or spoken hymn by the early church, is one of the most significant portraits of the person and work of Christ contained in the New Testament. Here the unshakeable foundation of Christian salvation and spirituality stands theologically elegant above all, like the Eiffel Tower in Paris. Notice how many times *he is* appears. *He is* the image of the invisible God (v. 15); *he is* before all things, and in him all things hold together (v. 17); *he is* the head of the body, the church (v. 18); *he is* the beginning and the firstborn from among the dead (v. 18). Notice the actions of Christ: *by* him all things were created . . . *by* him and for him (v. 16); *in* him all things hold together (v. 17); *through* him to reconcile to himself (God) all things. Note more key terms: *in everything*, he might have the *supremacy* (v. 18) and God was *pleased* to have all his *fullness dwell in him* (v. 19). How might your reflection on this passage about the Lord Jesus Christ impact in a tangible way, your group, church, or individual life? Do you get the impression, as Rick Warren announces in the *Purpose-Driven Life*, "It's not about you"?

Christ is the pre-existent Creator, Sustainer, Redeemer, and resurrected Lord of all creation and the church. He is an icon, a visible image of the invisible God who dwells in him fully and whom Jesus represents exactly. He holds a position of absolute prominence and power as God's Son and the world's Savior, who died on a cross to reconcile and make peace between God and all things. Christ is the *beginning* . . . and he is *supreme*. God is *pleased* to have all his fullness live in him (v. 19). Who is Jesus Christ? He's the sovereign Lord! He's the Ruler, Master and Commander of the universe. He's "the boss of you." He's God.

Like the massive liquid fuel that rumble thrusted the space shuttle into the heavens, these six verses contain enough massive theological fuel to thrust our spiritual life into holiness. Paul notes, "But now he has reconciled you by Christ's physical body through death to present you *holy* in his sight, without blemish and free from accusation—if you continue in your *faith*, established and firm, not moved from the *hope* held out in the gospel" (Col 1:22–23). The previous point is clear and compelling—Jesus is the beginning; he is supreme. He's God in human form. All of creation and the church exist by him, through him, and for him. The Roman emperors stamped their images on imperial coins to announce their lordship and supremacy. But Christ is the supreme image of God, in whose image we are being renewed (Col 3:10). As his followers, he stamps his image on us so people will see his lordship as we live in him. But living in the Lord means we will become *holy* as we continue in our *faith* not moved from our *hope* (sound familiar?). Holy in his sight, without blemish and free from accusation—like Job, who was a blameless man, with complete integrity, who feared God and avoided evil (Job 1:1).

Let's pause and reflect. Like a child who enters Disneyland for the first time, you may feel so overwhelmed and enthralled that you can hardly contain yourself and not know what to do. You may feel that you need to take time to study these theological truths in more detail. You may also feel that your spiritual life does not match the incomprehensible dimensions and standards that Paul writes about. And yet, you may feel challenged and excited about the adventure that lies ahead for your knowledge of Christ and your life in him. The journey to Jesus is like the journey to an academic degree—one course, one day, and one assignment at a time. Keep the goal in mind. Paul's purpose is to stretch our theological imaginations to a cosmic level, with the staggering implications for the universe itself from a colossal portrait of its Creator-Redeemer. Like the heart stirring Hallelujah Chorus in Handel's Messiah sung by a thousand-person choir, Paul's pastoral intent is to so enlarge our view of Christ that he dwarfs all else. King of kings and Lord of Lords, he shall reign forever and ever! Magnificent surrender . . .

Let's not reduce our faith to a mere doctrine about Christ. Rather, let's believe in Christ himself, the divine Person alive and active, who holds the universe and our life together. Daily, I try to orient myself toward Jesus like a compass orients itself toward magnetic north. Every morning I grab a cup of coffee and sit in my office in silence and solitude. I reflect on a Scripture passage in an attitude of submission often with a prayer of relinquishment. I pray for my family and for the day ahead of me. Regularly, I will also read from devotional works or use the *Sacred Space* website. My goal is to "pay absolute unmixed attention" to the presence and work of God in the daily rounds of my life. I notice the beauty in creation outside which points to the beauty of God himself. I pray for his guidance and wisdom and quiet my heart in his presence as I enter meetings with people. Then, I try and listen to people with my ears but listen to Jesus with my heart and mind, and so practice spiritual discernment and direction. As I move into a busy day, I face my own sin and the sin of others, and surrender to the reality that even in the midst of a broken world, Jesus is Lord. When I tire, I'm not as alert to listen to the Holy Spirit. I try to be aware of how someone or something can "push my buttons" where I need to prayerfully practice self control and "let it go."

I practice *faith thinking* as I muster Scripture into a conversation with the events of life, culture, and ministry around me, especially when I watch TV, which is full of sensual and consumer-driven messages. When my emotions are fearful or anxious, I pray to Jesus and sometimes recite the Jesus prayer: "Lord Jesus Christ, Son of God, have mercy on me, a sinner." When I feel a gnawing need to control situations, I try to affirm that *he* holds all things together and *he* is the head of his church. I recall Paul's words, that it's "Christ in me, the hope of glory" (Col 1:27). He is . . . the beginning . . . and also . . . the end.

THE END

I teach that people and churches should develop a short, memorable, mission statement and then develop measurable strategies and action plans to accomplish it. The leadership literature differentiates mission and vision, goals and actions, values and practices. However, I wonder if we can downsize the theological dimension of mission and spirituality with an overemphasis on modern organizational leadership. I still think we should be clear on our mission and values, but I wonder if we overrate them. To run the organization like *professionals* (which we are not), we can spend all our time and energy on budgets, staffing, buildings, programs, administration, and fund-raising, with endless meetings and long agendas. Leaders must focus on people development, spiritual oversight, prayer, and the Word. It seems the early apostles boiled it down to two absolutes: "We will give our attention to prayer and the ministry of the word" (Acts 6:4). I was to teach at a rural church about an hour west of Edmonton. I emailed the pastor and asked if he could send me his church's mission statement. He surprised me with this reply: "On paper we don't have a mission statement. In practice our mission statement is Matthew 28:19–20: make disciples; love God; teach the Word; obey Christ." Pretty simple, eh? By the way, this church is spiritually mature. In many ways, it's a group of people who are living in the Lord, who practice theology—Colossians style.

In the same year, I taught a seminary course on Colossians and then a college course on Pastoral Ministry. In both cases, in my preparation, one verse in Colossians 1 captured my imagination. I think it reflects Paul's mission statement for life and ministry. It's grounded in a theological focus for discipleship and spiritual formation. It should serve as the goal or purpose of pastoral leadership and for Christian spirituality. Here it is. When you can, read it carefully in several translations and let it germinate in your heart and mind. It is Colossians 1:28, "We proclaim him, admonishing and teaching everyone with all wisdom, so that we may present everyone perfect in Christ."

Paul's mission was to proclaim, admonish (warn), and teach everyone with all wisdom to present everyone *perfect* (mature, complete) in Christ. This is missional discipleship and spirituality. Then in verse 29 he writes, "To this end I labor, struggling with all his energy, which so powerfully works in me." It was to that *end* (goal and direction) that Paul struggled with Christ's energy to accomplish. What was the end or goal? To present everyone *perfect in Christ*. The word for perfect is *teleion*, derived from *telos*, which means end or goal. When something reaches its end or goal, it's considered mature, complete, finished, or perfect. Like an Olympic runner who struggles and agonizes with physical energy to reach the end, Paul struggles and agonizes with Christ's energy to reach the end—to present everyone *mature* in Christ.

Colossians 1:28–29 speaks of missional discipleship and Christian spirituality. The end is maturity in Christ. Twice Paul mentions that this is for *everyone* not just for the super-dedicated. The goal of Christian leadership is to proclaim, admonish, and teach with all wisdom so that people become mature in Christ. That is the goal or missional outcome of ministry. Spiritual formation involves Spirit-enlivened practices in discipleship to help shape Christ followers into his image, as they bear his character and participate in his mission. Discipleship is not a program to bolt onto church ministry or a class for new believers, but the very heart of church ministry. It's a relentless shaping of our destiny (*telos*) toward Christ-likeness.

This is a huge disconnect currently in many churches. We might say the mission of our church is to make disciples and yet are we clear on what it means to be a disciple and how to make one? To make matters worse, our consumer culture works hard to disciple us in spending, sensuality, and selfishness. The relentless messages in popular culture through TV, movies, music, the Internet, and advertising, undermine Christian virtue. Our consumer culture is a powerful shaping force that disciples us. A Jesus follower must learn to live in the world while not of the world as a counter-cultural *subversive*. I feel the worldly gravitational pull every time I enter a shopping mall or watch *Entertainment Tonight*. The constant allure of *buy* and *beauty* can create a gnawing dissatisfaction in me. Paul's comment is timely for me—what about you?

> For I have learned to be content whatever the circumstances. I know what it is to be in need, and I know what it is to have plenty. I have learned the secret of being content in any and every situation, whether well fed or hungry, whether living in plenty or in want. I can do everything through him who gives me strength. (Phil 4:11–13)

Jesus gave us the commission to go and make disciples of all people groups, baptizing (initiating) them into the name and life of the Trinity and teaching them to *obey* all that he commanded. Discipleship is really an *apprenticeship* in what it means to obey Jesus and become like him in our beliefs, values, lifestyle, and surrender to the will of the Father. We are clear on the *telos* of a four-year apprenticeship program as an electrician, mechanic, or carpenter. Are we as clear on the *telos* of a life-long apprenticeship process as a disciple—a learner and follower of Christ

Jesus the *Lord* in all of our life? Perhaps we have an identity crisis. Mark Sayers observes:

> *All our attempts to reshape the Church in the West will at best be sabotaged and at worst fail because there is a huge unnamed problem with people inside the Church.* As I traveled around speaking at churches of all sizes and approaches, I noticed that despite their completely different approaches, they had a common problem. It did not matter if the church was a small, emerging missional community; a traditional liturgical church on the corner; or a multisite contemporary megachurch. There was a basic problem of discipleship. The best way to describe the problem was to say that it was a crisis of identity.[2]

Discipleship isn't mere attendance at Sunday services. Someone wrote on *Facebook*: "We have to move beyond this idea that the once a week church gathering is the event where we really plug into God and get charged, then leave and try to run off that charge for the next 6 1/2 days." Discipleship is not an eight-week class either. It's a life journey toward Jesus as the end or goal, not separated into categories of evangelism (get saved) and then discipleship (get sanctified). If Paul declares that Jesus is the end goal of his preaching and teaching energy, should we do any less? I suggest we study all the passages in the Gospels where Jesus teaches on what it means to be a disciple and list all his commands and use these as our curricula. Then devote ourselves to prayer and the ministry of the Word in our small groups, Sunday services, staff, committee, board meetings, and programs, and organize around mission and discipleship.

This is the core of a *Lord-driven life*, which as apprentice-learners, we imitate and cling to the character, teachings, lifestyle, and mission of our Master. John places our future destiny in Christ as an incentive for present purity: "Dear friends, now we are children of God, and what we will be has not yet been made known. But we know that when he appears, we shall be like him, for we shall see him as he is. Everyone who has this hope in him purifies himself, just as he is pure" (1 John 3:2–3). What is the purpose of your life, your leadership, and your church? Where you start and where you finish, Christ is the beginning and the end, in our souls.

---

2. Sayers, *The Vertical Self*, xviii (italics in the original).

Have you ever heard of Henry Scougal? Scougal (1650–1678) was a devout Scottish Puritan who produced a number of works in his brief life while a pastor, and professor of divinity at King's College, Aberdeen. His greatest and lasting achievement was a book called *The Life of God in the Soul of Man*, originally written to explain Christianity and give spiritual counsel to a friend of his. This short treatise displays unusual theological perception and spiritual maturity for such a young adult. Scougal was noted for his piety and his clear grasp of Scripture, aided by his proficiency in Latin, Hebrew, Greek, and some oriental languages.

A year after the publication of *The Life of God in the Soul of Man*, Scougal died from tuberculosis at the age of only twenty-eight. A half century later, his treatise would profoundly influence such notables as George Whitefield and John Wesley. John Piper comments, "There are some books whose vision is so deep and clear that truth rings from the pages like the toll of a large bell, perfectly obvious, but rare and precious. They unfold the heart of man and God with such forceful illumination that the truth is not just shown to my mind but created in my heart."[3] Scougal wrote, "True religion is a union of the soul with God, a real participation of the divine nature . . . or, in the Apostle's phrase, it is Christ formed within us." He goes on to expound:

> The root of the divine life is faith; the chief branches are love to God, charity to man, purity, and humility: for, as an excellent person hath well observed, however these names be common and vulgar, and make no extraordinary sound, yet do they carry such a mighty sense, that the tongue of man or angel can pronounce nothing more weighty or excellent. Faith hath the same place in the divine life, which sense hath in the natural, being indeed nothing else but a kind of sense, or feeling persuasion of spiritual things; it extends itself unto all divine truths; but in our lapsed estate, it hath a peculiar relation to the declaration of God's mercy and reconcilableness to sinners through a Mediator; and therefore, receiving its denomination from that principal object, is ordinarily termed faith in Jesus Christ.[4]

Living in the Lord—the union of the soul with God and Christ formed within us—is rooted by faith in Jesus Christ with the chief branches of love to God and people, purity, and humility. Sustained with

---

3. John Piper, Amazon.com editorial review on *The Life of God in the Soul of Man*.
4. Scougal, *The Life of God in the Soul of Man*, 48.

a magnificent surrender, it all begins and ends with Jesus, who is . . . Perhaps you'd like to pray Henry Scougal's prayer of surrender:

> Infinite and eternal Majesty! Author and Fountain of being and blessedness! How little do we poor sinful creatures know of thee, or the way to serve and please thee! We talk of religion, and pretend unto it; but, alas! how few are there that know and consider what it means! How easily do we mistake the affections of our nature, and issues of self-love, for those divine graces which alone can render us acceptable in thy sight! It may justly grieve me to consider, that I should have wandered so long, and contented myself so often with vain shadows and false images of piety and religion; yet I cannot but acknowledge and adore thy goodness, who hast been pleased, in some measure, to open mine eyes, and let me see what it is at which I ought to aim. I rejoice to consider what mighty improvements my nature is capable of, and what a divine temper of spirit doth shine in those whom thou art pleased to choose, and causest to approach unto thee. Blessed be thine infinite mercy, who sentest thine own Son to dwell among men, and instruct them by his example as well as his laws, giving them a perfect pattern of what they ought to be. O that the holy life of the blessed Jesus may be always in my thoughts, and before mine eyes, till I receive a deep sense and impression of those excellent graces that shined so eminently in him! And let me never cease my endeavours, till that new and divine nature prevail in my soul, and Christ be formed within me.[5]

REFLECTION FOR GROUPS AND INDIVIDUALS

1   Let each person share with the others, or you personally reflect on, your spiritual journey from darkness to light, and on this text: "But you were washed, you were sanctified, you were justified in the name of the Lord Jesus Christ and by the Spirit of our God." Then share or reflect on group or personal applications of this quote: *"We can no longer live as we once did because we are no longer the people we once were."*

2. Read Colossians 1:15–20 in several translations and consult a few commentaries. Seek to paraphrase it and draw out the meaning of the deep truths contained in this Christological text. Reflect as a group or as an individual on how Christ's supremacy addresses you

5. Ibid., 58.

in terms of your group, church, and your personal life in the Lord. Notice the statements, "He is . . ."

3. Read Colossians 1:28–29 in several translations and consult a few commentaries. Seek to paraphrase it and draw out the central meaning. What is the significance of Christ as the *telos* (end, goal) of Christian maturity? How might this text serve as the purpose or philosophy of discipleship statement for all pastors, churches, and people? How is this related to being a subversive who counter-acts the shaping force of consumerism at the core of our culture?

PRACTICE FOR GROUPS AND INDIVIDUALS

1. As a group or individual, memorize Colossians 1:15–20. Rehearse it regularly, perhaps on a Monday morning to set the tone for your theological imagination for the coming week. Seek to carry these truths in your heart as you pray to Jesus as a group and as an individual. "Pay absolute unmixed attention" to his presence in your workplace and in your world.

2. Picture the end goal of what it would look like to be *mature* (perfect) in Christ, in your group, church, and individual life. Develop a working plan where your proclamation, admonishing, and teaching are all aligned to achieve this end goal. In other words, develop a discipleship strategy that you struggle with God to accomplish.

3. Read, weekly for six weeks, the full online version of Henry Scougal's, *The Life of God in the Soul of Man*. Notice the key ideas in each section. Summarize them in your own words. Pray his prayers at the end of each section. Seek to let your spiritual reading of Scougal shape your theological imagination and practice in your group, church, and personal life. For an online version see: http://www.ccel.org/ccel/scougal/life.i.html

3

Living in the Lord

"Live in me. Make your home in me just as I do in you."
(John 15:4, The Message)

A FEW YEARS AGO I read a book by Bob Buford called *Half Time*. It compelled me to reflect on and recalibrate my life. The basic point he makes is that there comes a place where our quest for success in the first half of our life must transition to a quest for significance in the second half. We enter a *mid-life* season in our lives he calls halftime. It's a time where we should review the first half so we might live the second half effectively. We must find the center and stay there, recalibrate our life mission, and then play for all we're worth. Soccer and football games are played in two halves. At halftime, the teams review how they played in the first half with the mission to win the game in the second half. All games are won in the second half. So is living in the Lord. *It's not how we start our life that counts, but how we finish.*

We all struggle to finish high school, attend college, land a good paying job, marry and start a family, buy a house, raise our kids, serve in our church, pay off the mortgage, and save for retirement. But that's not enough. Like a girl who longs for her wedding day, we long for and know deep inside that *we are made for something noble and transcendent.* As Hollywood celebrities confirm, fame and fortune, beauty and business, do not make a significant life. Someone said, "When you turn fifty, it's not the end of the world. But you can see it from there!" Solomon mused, "So, I'm all for just going ahead and having a good time—the best possible. The only earthly good men and women can look forward to is to eat and drink well and have a good time—compensation for the struggle for survival these few years God gives us on earth" (Eccl 8:15, *The Message*).

RICHES AND TREASURES

Struggle. Paul engaged in an intense struggle aimed at second half significance. The goal and end for which he struggled was to present everyone *mature* (perfect) in Christ (Col 1:28–29). Missional discipleship and spiritual formation for Jesus Christ was the mission of Paul's ministry and leadership. Dare we settle for less? He continued this struggle also for a *purpose*:

> I want you to know how much I am *struggling* for you and for those at Laodicea, and for all who have not met me personally. My *purpose* is that they may be encouraged in heart and united in love, so that they may have the full riches of complete understanding, in order that they may know the mystery of God, namely, Christ, in whom are hidden all the treasures of wisdom and knowledge. (Col 2:1–3)

The root word for *struggle* in this text and in 1:29 informs the English word, *agonize*. What does agonize mean? It means to persevere with intense struggle and effort. Why would Paul agonize so much for the Colossians and Laodiceans? He had a pastor's heart with a purpose in mind: that they would be encouraged in heart and united in love (v. 2). This is a key to effective ministry in the Lord, whether you serve as a pastor or as a layperson. My wife and I are friends of Luchie, a small Filipino Christian woman in Calgary who works in the heart and stroke field. She lost her husband to cancer not long after she and her three children immigrated to Canada. She has unwavering faith and a strong, though gentle, disposition. She helps other Filipino immigrants, opens her home to those who need a place to stay, distributes items for needy people, and offers support to single parents and other marginalized people. She struggles for all these people and more, as she also holds a demanding full-time job, serves as chair for our local church board, and serves on my district board. Through relentless purpose she keeps the end, the goal, the *telos*, in view—to encourage the hearts of others and unite them in love.

Paul struggled with a purpose, that all those people in verse 1 would be "encouraged in heart and united in love." What is the relationship between these and how do they provide essential ingredients for living in the Lord? We feel encouraged when we are in union with Christ and experience the comfort of his love, which flows from him and through his people one to another. We are conduits of Christ's love. Unity and encouragement thrive in relationships where we practice heart-warming love. You know what that feels like.

I came from a meeting with a church board and its pastor. The subject centered on what to do with another key board member and his wife who caused great trouble and disunity in the church. We discussed the issues and a meeting that the board had with this board member and his wife ten days before. The tone of that prior meeting was rather tense at the beginning, and our meeting also offered a few prickly moments. But as we talked and heard each other with love, the tone changed. The board members present at the previous meeting also remarked how the tone became softer when this couple humbled themselves after the board spoke the truth to them in love. Because of grace, we decided to give them another chance. As we progressed through the meeting, you could see and feel encouraged hearts, eye-twinkling laughter, with a united sense of love for each other, the church, and the couple. I slept a good eight hours that night!

We must assume that men and women *will* have conflict and disagreements in the church. Paul conflicted with Barnabas (Acts 15) and Euodia conflicted with Syntyche (Phil 4). It doesn't mean someone is wrong or bad or that godly Christians must avoid conflict at all costs. We view the world through our own eyes and assume others view it the same way. It's easy to judge people, dig in, and defend our own position like a soldier in a bunker. We can strain gnats and yet swallow camels while we break relationships and cement ourselves in pride. There are times to take a Scriptural or ethical stance, but often we can sweat the small stuff for the sake of principle and forget that love covers a multitude of sins. When we spend time together, tell our stories, have some fun, enjoy barbecues or potlucks, pray, and listen, we will get to know each other and learn to love and experience community. Conventional wisdom says, "Be kind, because everyone you meet is fighting a hard battle." When we have differences of ideas or instruction, we should seek to be knit together (of one mind) in love. This is at the heart of living in the Lord, and thus, Christian spirituality. Notice how Paul is consistent with these practices: "If you have any encouragement from being united with Christ, if any comfort from his love, if any fellowship with the Spirit, if any tenderness and compassion, then make my joy complete by being like-minded, having the same love, being one in spirit and purpose" (Phil 2:1–2).

Now watch the second half of the purpose for which Paul struggles. It gets even better: "So that they may have the full riches of complete understanding, in order that they may know the mystery of God, namely, Christ in whom are hidden all the treasures of wisdom and knowledge." Encouraged hearts united in love is a *community* practice that gains the riches of complete understanding that leads into the treasure house of all wisdom and knowledge hidden (stored) in Christ the Lord. Now this is real living in the Lord! As pastors and people, a key purpose for which we should *agonize* is to encourage the hearts of others and seek to unite them in love. As I've stated, Christian spirituality is *relational*. Love, as the fruit of the Spirit, results when people participate in the fellowship of the Spirit (see, Phil 2:1; 2 Cor 13–14).

People with encouraged hearts, who are united in love, somehow gain access *corporately* to inexhaustible treasures deposited and stored up in Christ. We need his wealth of wisdom and knowledge to thrive as faith communities. As Christian spirituality, this is relational and communal. Of course, people grow in spiritual formation through private disciplines, study, and union with Christ. But the practices of the faith community unleash the full riches of complete spiritual knowledge and wisdom. People in fellowship—who share a common spiritual life with each other in the Lord, encouraged and united in love—become receptive to the Lord and receptacles of the Lord through spiritual gifts and service to one another, exercised in love. When the church gathers, the spiritual gifts known as the word of knowledge and wisdom are available (1 Cor 12:8), as are prophecy, discernment, and teaching (12:9, 28). These offer godly insight and wisdom. The manifestation of the Spirit through spiritual gifts and the communication of revelation, become effective when exercised through love in a gathered setting (1 Cor 1314).

A problem in Colossae was that either the imperial Roman culture and/or false teachers mouthed off *fine sounding arguments* (Col 2:4) like the best-selling book or film entitled *The Secret*.[1] This led theologically naïve people to believe they could penetrate deeper mysteries or secret knowledge and wisdom through captivating philosophy or spirituality. The specific details emerge later in Colossians 2. Here's the issue: is Christ supreme and sufficient for all knowledge and wisdom? Where are true riches and treasures? God's true mystery is Christ, in whom all the treasures of knowledge and wisdom are stored. If you have a chance to

1. Byrne, *The Secret*.

visit the British Museum in London or the Louvre in Paris, do so. You can spend months there as you view, read about, and try to absorb the priceless treasures of the finest art and artifacts the cultures of the world have to offer. If you were to will the riches of the Rosetta Stone or the Mona Lisa to someone's inheritance, what would they be worth? For Jesus, the *priceless* riches of his glorious inheritance are in *us*, the saints (Eph 1:18).

I wrote today and then decided to take a break and head for the gym. As I swam laps in the pool, my mind swam circles in these truths. I thought: "You know Roger, you think a lot, study a lot, and you know a lot. For God's sake (literally), you have a doctoral degree in missional leadership and spiritual formation. Live up to the truth you already have. You lack a full understanding of Christ and don't always live according to the wealth of his wisdom and knowledge. You have control issues. You continue to be stubborn. You worry too much about money and at times overlook Jesus for wisdom. You read and read and don't consistently apply it to your life. You call others to a high standard of discipleship and mission; and yet, like a fizzled firecracker, you often fall short in your own life." Then I continued to muse in the hot tub. As I entered the dressing room, I read this sign on the door, "The greatest wealth is health."

I know what they mean, but that's not it. Yes, if we are disabled or lose our health, life can be tough where nothing else matters, not even a million bucks or a vacation cottage in Maui. But you and I both know wealthy *and* healthy people who live poverty-stricken spiritual lives. They have no true wealth even though they may earn six figure incomes, drive a BMW, frequent the gym, look like A-list celebrities, and play golf weekly. Then there are people that are not financially wealthy, but they might have a PhD or hold political office and view themselves as intellectually or socially wealthy. And yet, there are numerous PhDs and politicians whose lives are ramshackle messes collapsed into a heap of philosophical or moral ruin, devoid of wisdom.

Wisdom existed before creation, and then Christ placed wisdom into the very molecules of the creation itself (Prov 8). And "to fear the Lord is the beginning of wisdom, and knowledge of the Holy One is understanding" (Prov 9:10). We can find unlimited knowledge on the Internet or sit through hours of counseling. We can study and learn valuable biblical information or listen to Dr. Phil. But, unless we have a full understanding of Christ himself, all the treasures of knowledge and wisdom hidden in him will sit like unused coupons in an Entertainment book. Nothing compares and nothing competes. Wherever our treasure is, that's where the desires of our heart will also be. Is our heart set on Christ in whom all riches and treasures are stored? If so, we should delight to see how orderly we are and how *firm* our *faith* is in Christ (2:5). We end where we began: strong faith in Christ is the gateway to a rooted reception of Him as Lord.

RECEIVED AND ROOTED

Two significant words in the book of Colossians are hinge words: *so then*. When you hear the words *so then*, what do you hear, what connections do you make, what function do these words perform in a sentence? These conjunctions draw a conclusion, inference, or deduction, drawn from the previous theological discussion about the Lord Jesus Christ, supreme and sovereign Creator and Savior. Like a hinge, they swing back to draw the argument into a conclusion and then swing ahead to frame a new argument and application. They now bring us to the central message of Colossians and so, the message of my book. Read it carefully,

> So then, *just as you received Christ Jesus as Lord, continue to live in him*, rooted and built up in him, strengthened in the faith as you were taught, and overflowing with thankfulness. (Col 2:6–7)

Verse 6 serves as a hinge that swings the first section of the letter (Col 1:3—2:5) in the direction for all that follows in the second section (Col 2:7—4:6). Notice, we who *received* Christ Jesus as *Lord*, must continue to *live* in him. Let's explore what this means.

When Queen Elizabeth arrives in a country or attends an important event as an invited guest, what occurs? Let's take it further—what occurred when Princess Diana came to town? With any world-class person, what occurs is crowd crammed commotion, fascination, fanfare, and what we call a *royal welcome*! When a royal family member arrives, people welcome or receive them. There's often a formal reception. In many ways, people take members of the royal family to themselves. In fact, Diana was affectionately called "the people's princess." The marriage of her son, Prince William, to Kate Middleton, is the latest reception of royalty. This is exactly what we find in the phrase, *just as you received Christ Jesus as Lord*. This is a decisive, personal *and* corporate reception—to take Christ to us as the supreme sovereign. Paul draws together his theological treatment of who Jesus is and concludes, "So then, this is the Jesus Christ in whom you placed your faith and gave a royal welcome into your lives as Lord."

In his book, *The King Jesus Gospel*, Scot McKnight seeks to recover the original jam-packed and all-encompassing meaning of the gospel. It is more than simply the good news of an invitation to receive the forgiveness of sin, salvation, and then heaven through the Savior Jesus Christ. Rather, from the story of Israel right through the New Testament, the good news is the gospel of the kingdom of God, which focuses on the *lordship* of Christ Jesus. The proclamation of the gospel is a summons to repentance, faith, and then surrender and allegiance to Jesus as Messiah (Christ) and Lord. In its purest form, it is not a summons to receive Jesus as one's personal Savior. It is a costly call to discipleship, not a transactional call for a decision. He writes, "The messianic, lordly, and kingly confession of Jesus is not incidental to the Bible. It is the point of the Bible, and the gospel is the good news that Jesus is Messiah, that Lord, and that King. We are his subjects."[2] It is a decisive royal reception that lives on under his Kingship.

On this basis, don't end the royal reception; continue to live in him. We receive Christ Jesus as the Lord himself, not as a doctrinal statement or as a theological position. Paul's version of *receive* is an intensified form of what John meant when he said, "Yet to all who *received* him, to those who believed in his name, he gave the right to become children of God" (John 1:12). Here's the bottom line: after you receive Christ Jesus as Lord, *continue to live in him.* This has profound significance for Christian spirituality and discipleship. After you believe in Jesus you now behave in Jesus. Because you welcomed him, now walk with him. *Let go of control.* Continue the magnificent surrender—the sun-centered position of your spiritual solar system.

To *live* in him literally means to *walk* in him. This means to tread around or walk about. Paul uses the same word in Ephesians where he encourages, "I, therefore, the prisoner of the Lord, beseech you to *walk* (live) worthy of the calling with which you were called" (Eph 4:1, *NKJV*). This refers to the conduct of one's life. Annie Dillard wistfully mused, "How we spend our days is, of course, how we spend our lives."[3] How do you spend your days? Think of your family, your workplace, and

2. McKnight, *The King Jesus Gospel*, 141.

3. Dillard, *The Writing Life*, 32.

your community. Each day is a snapshot or a scene that will comprise a photo album or a feature film of your whole life. Will people see the Lord there?

We walk around as we walk with and in Christ as Lord. A decade ago, I wrote a book entitled, *The Journey: Walking with God*. What drove me was the question: what does it mean to walk with God? The Bible notes two people known for this, Enoch (Gen 5:22–24) and Noah. Let Enoch's great grandson Noah inspire you, "Noah was a righteous man, blameless among the people of his time, and he walked with God" (Gen 6:9). As if being righteous and blameless were not enough, Noah also walked with God! This refers to impeccable character and conduct forged by intimate relationship with the Lord—the "Intel Inside" of Christian spirituality. To walk *with* God is to live *in* Christ as Lord. This is the CPU of life we must *continue* daily.

Continue to live in him. This is unfathomable. Like stock in God's kingdom, it pays compounding dividends of eternal life itself. What is living in the Lord? It's a journey into the eternal Trinity, into the Pacific Ocean vastness and the Grand Canyon splendor of knowing God through Jesus Christ. "Now this is eternal life: that they may know you, the only true God, and Jesus Christ, whom you have sent" (John 17:3)—missional spirituality from the inside out. Eugene Peterson in *The Message* captures the image well, "Live in me. Make your home in me just as I do in you" (John 15:4). In other words, live and lodge in Jesus just as he lives and lodges in us! Wow, Jesus lives in us? I wonder how he feels about his home. Is it comfortable, inviting, loving, and hospitable? Does he feel that "there's no place like home" in Roger? Paul presses this theology into service: "I have been crucified with Christ and I no longer live, but Christ lives in me. The life I live in the body, I live by faith in the Son of God, who loved me and gave himself for me" (Gal 2:20); and then: "For to me, to live is Christ and to die is gain" (Phil 1:21).

Do we, do I, really believe this? As I awake and then practice solitude and silence each morning, I try to center my thoughts on Christ, before I have coffee. I seek to daily love the Lord with all my heart and make my home in him as he makes his home in me. What do you imagine and feel when you read, "Make your home in me just as I do in you," and "So then, just as you received Christ Jesus as Lord, continue to live in him"? To live in Christ means to walk and talk with Him, and follow and submit to him as Lord. As we go about the daily routines of life—at work, in our families, our communities, and our personal lives—Jesus informs and guides our values, thoughts, decisions, and conduct. It means that we look to him for our spiritual needs, for knowledge and wisdom, and we join his mission in the world around us as missional disciples.

What do you see as you imagine yourself in magnificent surrender? I see myself bowed down with bent knees in the sand on a beach, arms uplifted, eyes fixed skyward, dressed in white, enshrouded in hues of yellow and red beams emanating from a tropical sunset. Daily, as a first rule of life in the morning, I pray to Jesus, read a portion of Scripture, and try to quiet my heart in silence and solitude. Throughout my day, I endeavor to "pay absolute unmixed attention" to the Lord in my thoughts, in my conversations with people, and in my decisions. I choose to trust Jesus—that he is Lord and ultimately responsible to govern my life. My goal each day, each moment, is to orient my thoughts around the Lord instead of the things around me. I try to practice "anti-anxiety" and thankfulness as I meditate on truths like Colossians 3:1–4. This is not easy. At times I have lots of static in my thoughts and emotions. It takes concentration.

Paul now identifies four steps in this walk that includes one step back and three steps forward. We continue to walk (live) in him "rooted and built up in him, strengthened in the faith as you were taught, and overflowing with thankfulness" (Col 2:7)—rooted, built up, strengthened, and thankful. The first step that began in the past with a faith commitment to Christ continues to affect the present—we were and are now *rooted* in him. Like the vine and branches parable, this is a living metaphor drawn from the world of horticulture. It seeks to lodge the truth in our imagination that in Christ we are deeply secured and nourished by him.

If you get a chance, visit Sequoia and King's Canyon National Parks in California, home of the giant sequoia trees. The sequoias have a wide spreading root system that grows twelve to fourteen feet deep, and whose roots can occupy over one acre of earth and contain over ninety thousand cubic feet of soil. The mass of matted roots and soil must secure and nourish a tree nearly three hundred feet tall and weighing nearly two million pounds. The largest tree on earth is the General Sherman. It's a majestic sequoia considered over three thousand years old. At 275 feet tall, it has a circumference of 102 feet, and a diameter of thirty feet at the base. At a height of one hundred eighty feet the General Sherman maintains a thirteen-foot diameter. It's the largest tree on earth because it contains the largest volume of wood of any tree. In 1987 it was estimated to contain 52,508 cubic feet of wood. As spiritual sequoias, we are rooted and established in Christ's love (Eph 3:17). Imagine the potential and the riches of your life in Christ.

Paul moves from the horticulture metaphor to a construction metaphor. After we are rooted, the next step is that we are built up in him. Like new house construction that starts with the foundation and is built upwards, we are built in him. As the living temple of God, the church is a spiritual house, composed of living stones, which are holy priests who live in him (1 Pet 2:5). This is a metaphor that advances our walk with Christ a step forward. The rootedness of past belief now supplies a foundation for present building: "having been firmly rooted and now being built up in him" (*NASB*). With secure roots, Jesus now constructs our life in him. He has the blueprint for your life and his church, and his construction is right on schedule. He never runs out of material and never makes a mistake. His intent is to build a church as a people group, not just as a group of individuals. The Lord lives in his temple, which is his body, the church.

The next step in the walk is: "strengthened in the faith as you were taught." The root and building metaphors gain a broader scope of meaning where now we are strengthened or *established* or *secured* in the faith taught to us. The faith is the content of Christian belief *about* Christ and the action of trust *in* Christ. Epaphras taught the Colossians the faith. Christian theology and faith lead to belief in Jesus Christ, the subject and object of faith. Christ is the center of our spiritual lives—not the Bible, not prayer, not worship, not the spiritual disciplines. When we know whom we believe and what we believe, we are established and secured in our walk with Christ as we continue to live in him as Lord. This is a present and ongoing experience where the truth in Christ establishes the entire framework and content of Christian spirituality.

The church must be a teaching community, not just a study or sermon center. I love to learn. I love theology and teaching. But the goal of Christian teaching is to establish Christ followers in the faith. Discipleship includes baptizing converts into the life of the Trinity and teaching them to *obey* the commands of Christ, the content of faith. What would happen if we closed our places of Bible *study* and re-launched them as places of Bible *obedience*? If we don't practice what we learn through obedience we don't really practice our faith. I taught a six-week church based course on Lifestyle Discipleship. As we explored Matthew 28:18–20 we noted that a significant part of the Great Commission is to teach people groups to *obey* all that Christ commanded. So, as a class, we went through the book of Matthew and noted every time Jesus gave a command. We assembled all these commands on six sheets of paper and distributed them to everyone. I said to them: "Here's our curriculum for discipleship. Let's try it for six weeks."

This isn't new, for Jesus taught: "You are truly my disciples if you *keep obeying* my teachings. And you will know the truth, and the truth will set you free" (John 8:31–32, *NLT*). And "If you *obey* my commands, you will remain in my love, just as I have *obeyed* my Father's commands and remain in his love" (John 15:10). Living in the Lord means we will continue to be established in the faith we were taught, with constant refreshers as we also learn to practice *faith thinking*. Perhaps we need a renewal of catechism within our specific traditions, where we learn a summary of Christian doctrine. For example:

The Anglican Catechism:

Q: What is the Christian hope?

A: The Christian hope is to live with confidence in newness and fullness of life, and to await the coming of Christ in glory, and the completion of God's purpose for the world.

The Baptist Catechism:

Q 39: What is sanctification?

A: Sanctification is the work of God's free grace by which we are renewed in the whole person after the image of God, and are enabled more and more to die unto sin, and live unto righteousness.

The Westminster Shorter Catechism (Reformed):

Q 1: What is the chief end of man?

A: Man's chief end is to glorify God, and to enjoy him forever.

Finally, we will continue to live in the Lord with the final step of "overflowing with thankfulness." This is literally *abounding in gratitude.*

The word for gratitude or thankfulness, *Eucharist*, literally means *well graced* (from benefits and blessings we receive). How does gratitude fit here? Go back to the chain of thought: as we received Christ Jesus as Lord, we are therefore to continue living in him, rooted, built up, strengthened, and now grateful. It doesn't get any better. When we gave Jesus a royal welcome by faith, he escorted us into his kingdom with its inexhaustible and priceless riches, and made all his treasures available to us. Nothing can root, build, and strengthen us any more than that. After you scale the summit, there's nowhere else to go, nothing else to do, except to take it all in and bow down in magnificent surrender!

This morning as I write, I look out my home office window at a faultless and serene scene. The whole neighborhood sits graced under a blanket of fresh gleaming snow that quietly descended on it last night. Just a week ago, my wife and I were in Southern California over the Christmas holidays to visit my mother. The scene there, after a week of record rain, was blue, sunny, pristine skies dotted with stately palm trees and snow capped mountains in the distance. Creation shouts, "The earth is the Lord's and radiates its vast beauty and riches!"

When beauty and riches captivate us, heart-swelling gratitude is a natural response. The physical riches are a sacred glimpse, perhaps an icon, of the spiritual riches hidden in the Lord. Because Christ is the source of all beauty and wealth, gratitude is a way to acknowledge him, and a natural part of what it means to live in the Lord. When we express gratitude in abundance, we practice the sacrament of *Eucharist*. Gratitude is a response to grace, an attribute of God. Jesus often gave thanks and set the framework for the Lord's Supper or the *Eucharist*, as he gave thanks for the bread and the cup (Matt 26:26–27). Thanksgiving is a theme in Colossians and in the New Testament. Sense Paul's tone when he writes, "Be joyful always; pray continually; *give thanks* in all circumstances, for this is God's will for you in Christ Jesus" (1 Thess 5:16–18).

Our lives and lips must resound with the chorus and choreography of thanksgiving. The charming ambience of gratitude is an attitude that's basic to spirituality. It's a theological practice. When we view life through a lens that detects God's grace we must give thanks. If we fail to thank God, it can result in futile thinking and a darkened heart, "For although they knew God, they neither glorified him as God nor gave thanks to him, but their thinking became futile and their foolish hearts were darkened" (Rom 1:21). Part of my rule of life and leadership is to daily name five things for which I am grateful to God. C. Neil Strait mused, "Thanksgiving puts power into living, because it opens the generators of the heart to respond gratefully, to receive joyfully, and to react creatively."[4] Pray through Ralph Waldo Emerson's words:

> For flowers that bloom about our feet,
> For tender grass so fresh and sweet,
> For the song of bird and hum of bee,
> For all things fair we hear or see,
> Father in heaven, we thank Thee.
>
> For blue of stream and blue of sky,
> For pleasant shade of branches high,
> For fragrant air and cooling breeze,
> For beauty of the blooming trees,
> Father in heaven we thank Thee.
>
> For this new morning with its light,
> For rest and shelter of the night,
> For health and food, for love and friends,
> For everything Thy goodness sends,
> Father in heaven, we thank Thee[5]

REFLECTION FOR GROUPS AND INDIVIDUALS

1. Read Colossians 2:1–3 in several translations and consult a good commentary. How do you as a group, church, or individual release the full riches of complete understanding to know Christ in whom are hidden (stored) all the treasures of wisdom and knowledge? How does Paul's purpose become a strategic purpose for us all? How does that work practically?

2. Look up the word *Lord* in a Bible dictionary. What does it mean? What is its significance in light of the Roman culture around Colossae? How would you translate the word *Lord* over into your culture with the same weight of meaning? Paul gets to the heart of the cultural and theological issue when he says, "Just as you re-

4. Cory, *Quotable Quotations*, 396.

5. Emerson, "Father I Thank Thee." Online: http://www.desertwebcenter.com/we _thank_thee.html.

ceived Jesus as *Lord*, continue to live in him" (as Lord). How would you answer the question, what does it mean that Jesus is Lord?

3. Read Colossians 2:6–7 in several translations and consult a good commentary. How does this text serve as a hinge for what precedes and then for what follows? In your own words, paraphrase and summarize what this text actually says. What does it mean to live (walk) in him, and how do being rooted and built up, strengthened in the faith, and overflowing with thankfulness (gratitude) flow out of this? How would this text work as a charter for your group, church, or individual life?

PRACTICE FOR GROUPS AND INDIVIDUALS

1. Daily recite the Great Commandment, "Hear, O Israel, the Lord our God, the Lord is one. Love the Lord your God with all your heart and with all your soul and with all your mind and with all your strength . . . Love your neighbor as yourself" (Mark 12:29–30). Seek practical ways to express your spirituality from the inside out.

2. Make it a disciplined practice to always find a way to encourage hearts and unite in love, and then pay attention to how the riches of a full understanding to know Christ and his treasures of wisdom and knowledge are released to your group, church, or to you as an individual.

3. Daily practice gratitude. Observe life around you and detect glimpses of God's beauty and grace. Rather than complain or criticize, ponder Annie Dillard's words, "How we spend our days is, of course, how we spend our lives."

4

Christians and Culture

"No culture has appeared or developed except together with a religion: according to the point of view of the observer, the culture will appear to be the product of the religion, or the religion the product of the culture."[1]

I'M CONVINCED THAT ONE of the toughest jobs on the planet is parenting. With three grown children to our credit—one daughter and two sons—a friend's words ring in my memory: "When your children are little you talk to them about God. When they are teens you talk to God about them!" When our kids entered elementary school, they listened to my wife and me. When they entered middle school, they listened to their friends. And they all listened to the values and cravings of pop culture. The word *angst* describes how we felt as parents—due to the barrage of captivating cultural influences hurled at our kids from certain movies and music, drugs and alcohol, sensuality, and peer attachment. These were also vexed with pop culture's philosophy of personal choice and general disrespect for the values of family, church, and authority.

Similarly, I'm further convinced that one of the toughest battles on the planet is being a Christ follower. Like middle school teens adrift in a rudderless boat tossed back and forth by cultural waves, many Christians continue to be "tossed back and forth by the waves, and blown here and there by every wind of teaching" (Eph 4:14; Jas 1:6). Attractive assaults on the truth of Jesus Christ as Lord continue to captivate well-meaning Christians today as they did in the days of the Colossians. Paul warned, "See to it that no one takes you captive through hollow and deceptive

---

1. Eliot, *Christianity and Culture*, 87.

philosophy, which depends on human tradition and the basic principles of this world rather than on Christ" (Col 2:8). We all hold a view of the world, and culture is a shaping force in what we see. Hollow and deceptive, human and worldly philosophy does not surrender to Christ.

HOLLOW PHILOSOPHY

As a second-year college student, I enrolled in Philosophy 101. It was a fascinating course that introduced me to age-old questions about the meaning of life and how we know. The first quote I learned from Greek philosopher Socrates was, "The unexamined life is not worth living." I also learned the core teachings of other sages like Plato, Descartes, and Kant, whose views continue to exert influence in our world today. There's a valid place to study philosophy and learn from classical thinkers. But we also have our own pop philosophers like Oprah who tell us how to "live your best life" and sages like the Dalai Lama who teach us "the way to freedom". Like a gravitational force field, religious longings ever draw people's hearts to explore philosophy and spirituality. The word *philosophy* means *love of wisdom*. But as we learned in Colossians 2:3, it's "Christ in whom are hidden all the treasures of wisdom and knowledge." Paul declares this "so that no one may deceive you by fine-sounding arguments" (2:4).

Hollow philosophy, deception, and fine sounding arguments, birthed in humanistic and worldly ideas and values, constantly blitz into people's hearts and minds. That's a daunting arsenal for Christians to constantly ward off. The relentless barrage of materialistic and sexual advertising, movies, music, television, celebrityism, and consumerism, allures and shapes our hearts, our loves, and our imaginations about "the good life" or "the American dream." *American Idol*, Ellen DeGeneres, *MTV*, *The View*, *New York Times* bestsellers, and Hollywood, to name a few, offer enough hollow philosophy and spirituality to derail the best-intentioned Christian. These cultural communicators are not always evil or wrong, but they often promote unbiblical and fine sounding worldly arguments. The question at stake is this: is Jesus Christ supreme and sufficient to sustain our lives? Must we add human traditions and the basic principles of the world to Christ? Is Jesus Christ *Lord*? Will we continue to *live* in Him alone?

I have a friend who's been a Christian for quite awhile—a charming man married to a faithful woman. I always thought he lived life reasonably well through his ups and downs. Because we moved away from British Columbia to Alberta I'd not seen him for a couple of years. So I sent him an email to ask how his soul was. Here's his reply:

> You asked me how is my soul. Well the past six months have been the darkest in my 57 years on this earth. I have been very depressed with life and money and my faith went south when I was angry with God. I had not felt him until two weeks ago when I tried to take my life with an overdose of booze and prescription drugs and putting a rope around my neck in the woods off and on for 8 hours choking and releasing it before I passed out. I lay on the floor of the forest listening to Satan that I would be better off dead. I put my wife through hell that day and she didn't know if I was dead or alive. I finally called her and told her I couldn't go through with it and drove back where she met me and then to have the police meet me to commit me to the locked up nut ward for two weeks. They moved me to a step house for recovery.
>
> God took me to my darkest hour and he showed himself to me and I have never felt his love and presence the way I feel him now. A friend said, "God never wastes a hurt!" I have been going to AA six days a week the past two weeks. A friend told me about a program from Saddleback Church called Celebrate Recovery. I feel very directed with my wife to start a group here that is about hurts, habits and hang-ups and it is based upon the beatitudes. God will use my past to his glory and to help people. I just ministered yesterday to a friend that had a gun to his head two weeks ago. God has done a 360 in my life the past two weeks. I pray now everyday that his will be done in our lives and in everything I do for his glory. I'm God's original masterpiece and he has favor on me.[2]

My friend, who'd suffered with depression, drinking, and personal bankruptcy, could not find a way to cope with his pain and disappointment in life. He also explored *The Secret*, a New Age philosophy based on the law of attraction. It teaches that how we think can attract our wishes and success into existence. My friend believes in Jesus, but belief isn't enough. He must translate belief in Jesus as Savior into magnificent surrender to Jesus as *Lord*, and continue to *live* in him alone. We all develop different coping mechanisms to manage our pain. People will eat, work, spend, exercise, indulge, and meditate for personal fulfillment.

---

2. Used by permission.

To fill our voids, our culture offers an array of hollow *consumption* and *production* options rather than Christ.

I've taught a Bible college course on worldviews. In the course, we explore various worldviews and philosophies and how people seek to satisfy their longings and purpose with sources outside of Christ. People become entangled in relentless drives to experience an abundant life through ways that never quench their thirsty souls. A thirsty soul will look to money, drugs, alcohol, sexuality, power, work, entertainment, philosophies, and even spirituality or love for satisfaction. I asked our class a question: "Why do people return over and over to things that never satisfy?" One very perceptive female student replied: "It's because they never satisfy." That was a God moment for me!

Now here's why we shouldn't rely on fine sounding *human* philosophies to fill us up: "For in Christ all the fullness of the Deity lives in bodily form, and you have been given fullness in Christ, who is the head over every power and authority" (Col 2:9–10). This theological statement advances our knowledge of Christ to the Library of Congress proportions. If all the fullness of God lives in him and he's the head over every power and authority, he's King of the mountain and the highest court of appeal in the universe. You can't skyrocket any higher than Christ. And here's the application: "You have been given fullness in Christ!"

Human philosophies are as hollow, empty, and inglorious as Niagara falls would be if drained of their water. Christian faith contains the Pacific Ocean fullness of Christ himself, who is God incarnate. The world's traditions and teachings cannot fill, cannot satisfy, cannot liberate. Any substitute or addition to Christ himself reduces him to a mere prince when he's the King of Kings and Lord of Lords. Like the insatiable appetite of an alcoholic or addict ruthlessly compelled to consume more to satisfy their craving, deceptive philosophies over promise and never deliver. The reason is because there's a *spiritual* power behind the disguise. The ancients, as many cultures today, associated spiritual beings with the basic principles or elements of the world. In a sense, any humanistic and deceptive philosophy of the world is *demonized*.

Fullness in Christ, due to your union with him, is a gift you didn't earn and don't deserve. It's a permanent gift of God's grace with continuous results. Just as you *received* Christ you must continue to *live* in him. The totality and entirety of who He is—with all his riches and treasure— are available to you when you practice a magnificent surrender to him as

Lord. "In him," Paul continues, "you were also circumcised, in the putting off of the sinful nature . . . having been buried with him in baptism and raised with him through your faith in the power of God, who raised him from the dead" (Col 2:11–12). Let's ponder this theology.

The mother lode of Christian theology is *Christology*—the person and work of Christ. It's hard to fathom these ancient truths packed into a short letter originally read out loud to the Colossian church, located in a small rural outpost in what's now western Turkey. I've served as a church layman, Bible College and seminary instructor, pastor, denominational leader, author, and church consultant. I know Christian theology. I read voraciously and I vigorously try to cultivate my spiritual life. I pray, read Scripture, attend church, and seek to include God in my values and decisions. And yet in my world, now two thousand years away from Colossae, as I type away on my MacBook Pro in my home near Calgary, with Internet access in the background and Starbucks coffee in my mug, I feel at times I'm merely one thin ice choice away from ruin. Though I've died to my former pagan life of lying, lust, and languish, it hasn't died to me. My anxiety and angst if not slain daily, can master me.

How can good churchgoing people who read their Bibles and pray, when overcome with calamity or consternation, choose to grab the bottle, watch soap operas, surf internet porn sites, drain their bank account, cash in their marriage for a one night fling, or pop pills to end it all? Theological answer: just as they received Christ Jesus as Lord, they did *not* continue to live in him. Practical answer: they did not practice a magnificent surrender. Some cheap lie, some habitual pattern, some coping tool, or some hollow and deceptive philosophy, sent their soul to the "dark side of the force," which betrayed and blackened them. An applied Christology is the only answer. We must choose to live in the reality of which Paul writes. If I don't *daily* monitor my thoughts, and declare *no* to lust and pride with a simultaneous *yes* to Jesus as Lord of my whole life, I could careen over the edge into an immoral or unethical canyon like a top heavy bus traversing a steep and narrow mountain road in Thailand. God help me! How about you?

I know that how we make choices is complex. Depression and anger, suicidal thoughts, personality and eating disorders, control issues, and addictions of all brands, are not easily dislodged from people's lives. It's difficult for *me* to change! Sin, which plagues the human race, runs as deep and steep as the Grand Canyon. And yet a theological, though real, transaction occurred for us in Christ's crucifixion and resurrection. We died and were raised with him. How? I don't know, but somehow in our union with Christ by faith, we participated in his journey. Our water baptism (spiritual circumcision) is the theological image of that journey: in Christ we submerged, cut off, and buried the old life as a sinner. We emerged, raised and renewed as a saint, by faith in the power of God who raised Jesus from the dead. *We therefore can no longer live as we once did because we are no longer the people we once were.* It goes further:

> When you were dead in your sins and in the uncircumcision of your sinful nature, God made you alive with Christ. He forgave us all our sins, having canceled the written code, with its regulations, that was against us and that stood opposed to us; he took it away, nailing it to the cross. And having disarmed the powers and authorities, he made a public spectacle of them, triumphing over them by the cross. (Col 2:13–15)

Notice God's actions: God made you alive, forgave, canceled, took away, nailed, disarmed, made a public spectacle, and triumphed! Do you ever feel like God is distant, quiet, and inactive? Do you ever feel like prayer, Bible reading, spiritual disciplines, and your Christian faith, simply don't work because God's passive? Do you ever feel that your spiritual life is like Kirstie Alley who, after being fired as a promoter of Jenny Craig, gained eighty-five pounds because she lost the accountability and focus? God is always active. He takes the initiative. Christmas and Easter were not festive holidays for God. Everything was at stake in these cosmic battles that remedied forever the fate of lost people consigned to the Devil's dungeons. Too much is at stake for God to not actively spend the infinite investment of his Son's life on you. That's why he commissioned Paul to write such a rainbow brilliant letter to a church of struggling Christians in a small town, compromised and oppressed by demonic philosophy.

God permanently disarmed the deceitfulness of these powers and authorities and shamed them publicly with his triumph by the cross of Christ. They still continue to influence worldly aspects of today's cultures, but like toothless, hairless, junkyard dogs, they now have more hoarse bark than bite. It all started with *God made you alive.* That means beforehand you were dead! Back to the point of Colossians: "Just as you received Christ Jesus as *Lord,* continue to *live* in him"—even if you've gained back some sluggish pounds of unfocused spiritual frustration.

Christ has no rivals and needs no supplements. He's active and alive; so don't settle for your culture's alluring un-spirituality.

UN-SPIRITUALITY

New Testament scholar Dean Fleming writes about a missionary colleague in the Philippines who described a chance encounter he had with a grandmother in a part of the country where local animistic religion was widely practiced. He noticed a cross hanging around her neck and asked if she was a Christian. "Yes," she assured him, "I'm a follower of Jesus Christ." When she discovered that his friend was a Christian missionary she invited him to visit her humble home. To his surprise, she showed him a traditional spirit house behind her home that was intended to ward off evil spirits. "If you are a Christian," he asked, "why do you still keep a spirit house?" Her matter-of-fact reply: "I just want to make sure that all of the bases are covered."[3]

It doesn't matter if you're a Christian in the Philippines or in Philadelphia, syncretism is a potent lure to "cover all the bases" when your view of Jesus Christ is shrunk, or when you've come out of a pagan background. Christians today can attempt to "cover all the bases" when they forfeit the riches of fullness in Christ for cheap materialism and New Age or pop spiritualities and sensualities showcased in day-time talk shows and steady diets of R-rated movies and music videos. Because we have "eternity written in our hearts" we long to live life in fullness, with power over and pleasure in our circumstances. C. S. Lewis suggested, "If I find in myself a desire that this world cannot fulfill, the most probable explanation is that I was made for another world."[4] All cultures express religion and spirituality in various forms. In Colossae, a complex smorgasbord of Greek, Roman, and Jewish philosophy, mysticism, legalism, and folklore competed with the simplicity of Christ and the gospel. Like London or Toronto, the Lycus valley was a busy intersection of various enmeshed cultures. The Colossians felt pressure to pledge allegiance to both Christ and the cultural powers and spirits. I wonder if we feel the same.

In the West, a significant cultural power that seeks our allegiance is the cult of *consumption*. We live in a consumer culture, where ad-

3. Fleming, *Contextualization in the New Testament*, 214.
4. Lewis, *Mere Christianity*, 121.

vertising and the idolatry of celebrityism and enjoying "the good life" constantly provoke our lusts and wants. Why do sports and movie celebrities fascinate us? Why are supermodels and actresses on the cover of most popular magazines? Why do we hustle the day after Christmas to jammed packed malls to take advantage of sales even though newly opened presents pack our living rooms? Why are so many overweight and in debt? Most of us likely have half a dozen credit cards, with lines of credit, loans, and mortgages. However, Solomon wrote, "Whoever loves money never has money enough . . . as goods increase, so do those who consume them" (Eccl 5:10–11). The cult of consumption, beauty, and prosperity compel many to feel they *must* have new homes, furniture, cars, computers, clothes, entertainment systems, time-shares, and new faces and bodies. The consumption chant is, "If I only made a little more; if I only looked like her, I'd be content."

Christians consume as much food and alcohol as non-Christians and Christians are often known as those who tip the worst at restaurants. The relentless drive to spend more and have more is shaped by ultimate concerns, governed by the deep religious and spiritual desires and loves in our lives. We become what we love. Our appetites for more are spiritual symptoms of a shrunken view of Christ. Paul teaches, "And you have been given fullness in Christ, who is the head over every power and authority" (Col 2:10). Christ's position and power are absolute, no one will every outrank him. All the fullness of Deity lives in him. Because we are in union with him, we have a permanent and continuous fullness as vast as the Pacific and Atlantic oceans.

My appetite for books, productivity, and food, mask a deeper hunger for *consumption* to feel in control with knowledge and to make things happen. For me, food can be a substitute anesthetic and reward where alcohol and drugs used to manage my anxieties. Because my pagan life involved voracious sensuality and self-indulgence, I realize I'm only one Internet mouse click or one liquor store away from an alluring trap. It's a daily discipline for me to say yes to the Lord and no to a culture of consumption. I see the same commercials and feel the same tug as you when I enter a mall. It's not wrong to buy stuff or upgrade to the latest iPhone. But is consumption a *master* or not? I must surrender my mind, emotions, eyes, and ears, to the Lord.

And yet, I can also be so frugal that I will lack generosity. This is just another expression of consumption based on a spirit of poverty where "one man gives freely, yet gains even more; another withholds unduly, but comes to poverty. A generous man will prosper; he who refreshes others will himself be refreshed" (Prov 11:24–25). As a spiritual discipline, my wife and I tithe my income and we give to people and causes as needs arise. But we must rely on the Lord and not our lusts to feed our life in him. Instead of a cult of consumption, which never satisfies, Jesus offers us the magnificent surrender that fed him, "My food is to do the will of him who sent me and to finish his work" (John 4:34). At the root is a spiritual hunger that only God can feed. When the devil tempted Jesus to compromise his forty-day fast with an unauthorized conversion and then consumption of stone turned to bread, he replied with eternal exactness. The Son of God cited Deuteronomy 8:3: "It is written: 'Man does not live on bread alone, but on every word that comes from the mouth of God'" (Matt 4:4).

Those in Asian, African, and Indian cultures live in an enchanted world of ancestor worship, divination, medicine men, shamans, and rituals designed to appease the spirits. Postmoderns live in a consumer world of "spirituality" and wellness they can grab to appease themselves. Unfortunately, like the Colossians, Christians today can grab the gray shadows over the full color reality found in Christ. Like mutant mystics, they can focus on food regulations, whether they work on "the Sabbath" or not, asceticism, angels, and visionary experiences (Col 2:16–18). Like the fastidious Pharisees and the meticulous Mishnah (a collection of Rabbinic oral tradition), Christians can obsess about rules and regulations that define so-called holiness and spirituality. They can fall into a fundamentalism and legalism so enthralled with the written Word that they deny the power thereof and know not the living Word. Or they can launch into a gnostic spirituality of charismatic experiences so enthralled with the Spirit that they know not the written Word. But with such "un-spirituality" Paul pronounces three indictments:

1. He has lost connection with the Head (Col 2:19). Jesus is no longer the life-giving source and substance of their spirituality.

2. These are all destined to perish with use, because they are based on human commands and teachings (Col 2:22). These are a religious humanism, finite, and temporary.

3. Such regulations indeed have an appearance of wisdom, with their self-imposed worship, their false humility and their harsh treat-

ment of the body, but they lack any value in restraining sensual indulgence (Col 2:23). Not regulated by Christ through the Spirit and the Word, these attempts at fullness never sanctify our sensual side.

Human driven syncretists, spiritualists, and legalists lose a vital connection with Christ and lack the capacity to restrain sensual indulgence. Paul connects your spirituality with your sensuality. Is it any wonder many Catholic priests and prominent evangelicals expected to model personal piety and bodily restraint could not tame the restless immoral monsters within themselves? It seems religious regulations designed to curb sensual desires actually heighten their power. Spiritual disciplines and religious rules can serve wholesome goals. But when elevated above Christ himself, they become the substance and Christ becomes the shadow.

If Christians add New Age, Buddhist, Hindu, Islamic, or postmodern spiritualities and idolatries to their faith and life in Christ, like the Israelites did with the Canaanites, they practice cultural syncretism. They can become a dead limb on a living body, detached from the Head. We cannot augment life in Christ with human spirituality no matter how fine sounding it is. Rather, "Since you died with Christ to the basic principles of this world, why, as though you still belonged to it, do you submit to its rules" (2:20)?

You don't need to become a fundamentalist and withdraw from your culture. Pharisees, monks, and Hutterites chose that path. When you withdraw from culture you still take your sin and sensual drives with you. To construct a refuge mentality to escape the corruption in "the world" is not the answer. You may have to say no to television or to certain channels, or alcohol, or credit cards, to guard your heart from certain temptations. But you have the fullness in Christ. You don't need to become a social activist and confront your culture. We must take a stand on moral issues and be responsible citizens to meet human need and serve our communities.

However, to promote a militant political or religious agenda like the Crusades or the Moral Majority will fail to transform culture enough that syncretism is not an issue in the church. Even though Constantine made Christianity the state religion for the Holy Roman Empire, history shows that if a Pope, Church, doctrine, or King shrinks the supremacy or sufficiency of Jesus Christ, raw evil will merely adorn itself in religious vestments. You don't need to become a liberal and accommodate your culture. In a pluralistic culture, Christians who want to practice "toleration" and "relevance" and not "judge others" can adapt Christian truth to the shifting waves of public opinion. To compromise with culture is not the path to relevance. Look at Jeremiah, John the Baptist, and Jesus for models of those whose agendas were counter-cultural and in many ways irrelevant, except in holiness, justice, love, and righteousness.

With Jesus Christ and his incarnation as your model, simply become salt and light and engage your culture. Be *in* but not *of* the worldly aspects of culture. Cultivate virtue and live as a child of light in the places of darkness where people will observe your character and conduct. Through a magnificent surrender, live in Jesus Christ as Lord. Let me introduce you to Sarah, a twenty-seven year-old Youth for Christ missionary to Calgary. One Sunday she preached in her home church where we attended. She delivered a power-packed message that rocked us all. Here's an excerpt:

> I want to talk to you today about *Jesus as Lord* and what that means for us. The word *Lord* refers to a master, to someone who has control, power, and authority over you. It's someone you serve and are accountable to. Shane Claiborne states that the root of the word *allegiance* means *lord*. Who has power and authority over you? Whom do you serve? To whom do you pledge allegiance?
>
> We in North America don't have a foreign power over us. But we are like the Israelites if we replace Christ as Lord with anything else—materialism, wealth, sex, safety, or security. We become Lord of our own lives when we serve ourselves and place our needs ahead of everything else. To serve Jesus as Lord will change the way we live. Matthew 6:24 declares that we can't serve two masters. If we aren't serving Jesus as Lord with our whole hearts, minds, and actions, we're not serving Him. A servant reflects his master. If Jesus is our master, our lives should reflect Him. The things that were important to Him should also be to us—feed the hungry; give to the poor; care for the sick, the widows, and the orphans; welcome strangers; love our enemies.
>
> Many overwhelming things occur in this world. How do we help the thirty-five thousand children who die daily of preventable causes? How do we stop the sex trade? Human trafficking brings in over three billion dollars in annual profit to traffickers. Worldwide, two thousand people commit suicide daily. In

the US alone, Americans spend four hundred billion dollars on Christmas gifts. I think that I'm too small to do *anything* about all this. I'm right. I'm very small. But my God is not. I serve a *risen* Lord who has all authority in heaven and on earth! Romans 8:31 trumpets, "If God is for us, who can be against us?" Verse 37 says, "In all these things we are more than conquerors through him who loved us." So how dare we sit passively and proclaim Jesus as Lord with our words and not follow Him with our actions. Show people that Jesus is Lord of your life by how you act, how you live, and how you speak with authority about what He's done for you. You will live a rich life.[5]

In the next chapter, you will see how this works out. It begins with a heavenly mind set on Jesus Christ who is supreme and all sufficient. It then becomes tangible and practical in the daily rounds of living in the Lord through a magnificent surrender. Danish Christian philosopher Søren Kierkegaard wrote a tractate entitled, "Purity of Heart is to Will One Thing." While I was a doctoral student in a course on spiritual formation, Dr. Phil Zylla asked us to compose a poetic prayer and share it. I entitled mine, "To Will One Thing." Perhaps you might want to pray it:

To Will One Thing

Teach me O Lord, to know your ways,
You who dwells in magnificent perfection,
Illumine my mind with resplendent beauty,
Formed, transformed to attend your will,
Renewed and readied to will one thing.

Guide me O Lord to follow your ways,
You who paces in eternal corridors,
Embolden my heart with steadfast longings,
Fearless, faithful to select your pleasure,
Restored and robust to will one thing.

Bless me O Lord to practice your ways,
You who rules in humble grandeur,
Inflame my will with impeccable delight,
Submitted, obedient to seek your face,
Responsive and resolved to will one thing,
A magnificent surrender.

---

5. Used by permission.

REFLECTION FOR GROUPS AND INDIVIDUALS

1. What's your view of culture? What are its challenges, its blessings, its curses for your Christian faith and life? How can your church, your group, or you as an individual engage culture with a lofty view of the Lord Jesus Christ?

2. What are some fine sounding philosophies based on human ideas and traditions that you have encountered? Why are they attractive and how are they deceptive? How can you evaluate them in light of your life in the Lord as a church, as a group, or as an individual?

3. How are you tempted to add to Christ to fill up your life? What are the implications of the truth that, *you have been given fullness in Christ*? What aspects of popular culture and media captivate you and why? What can you do to avoid syncretism as a church, as a group, or as an individual?

PRACTICE FOR GROUPS AND INDIVIDUALS

1. *Discern*: Memorize Colossians 2:8–10. Place this passage over your heart, mind, eyes, ears, and emotions. Practice biblical discernment in light of this passage with all movies, music, TV, advertising, Internet, books, magazines, and other cultural influences in your life.

2. *Decide*: Every morning set the course of your day with the determination that you will decide to say *no* to your tendency to look for ways to cope with your tensions and trials apart from Christ and to say *yes* to a magnificent surrender to live only in the Lord.

3. *Do*: Daily seek to practice the substance of love for God and others and do not get tangled up in the shadows of mutant mysticism or fastidious rule-keeping to regulate and define your holiness and spirituality.

5

Heavenly Minded for Earthly Good

*"We can't believe everything we see,
nor can we see everything we believe."[1]*

MOST OF US WILL acknowledge the power of a parent's words. I can remember several popular proverbs that my dad offered as conventional wisdom for life when I was a boy:

"Never tell a lie, because you'll have to remember what you said."

"If it's worth doing, it's worth doing right."

"Boys should never hit girls."

"A penny saved is a penny earned."

"You can do whatever you set your mind on."

Each one of these contains a noble truism, but as a goal oriented person, I've recently re-evaluated that last one. Over the years I've set my mind on many things: to earn academic degrees, invest, pay off our mortgage, learn to love my wife better, parent my children, be an effective leader, say no to lust and materialism, and now, to practice a magnificent surrender. However, there are things I simply can't do even if I set my mind on them: lose weight, play guitar like John Mayer, write like Eugene Peterson, or serve others as well as Mother Teresa. Furthermore, that last proverb is basically a humanistic one that focuses on *me*. I can make progress and focus on personal goals and self-improvement, but as Rick Warren reminds us in the *Purpose Driven Life*, "It's not about you!" If Jesus is Lord, and he occupies a sovereign place as the only one who is supreme and sufficient in all areas of my life, then it's about him, isn't it?

---

1. Donna Lowe on *Facebook*.

RAISED

In Colossians 3:1, Paul uses another hinge phrase, "Since, then . . ." He turns from his theological portrait of Jesus as *Lord* in chapters 1–2 to Jesus as *Life* in chapters 3–4 and how to practically live in him. It starts with a continuous and concentrated raised mindset on *him*. "Since, then, you have been raised with Christ, set your hearts on things above, where Christ is seated at the right hand of God. Set your minds on things above, not on earthly things. For you died, and your life is now hidden with Christ in God. When Christ, who is your life, appears, then you also will appear with him in glory" (Col 3:1–4). Are you wonder bursting about *glory*?

Our thoughts shape our theology and our spirituality, which shape our souls. Roman Emperor Marcus Aurelius (121–80 AD) stated, "Such as are thy habitual thoughts, such also will be the character of thy mind; for the soul is dyed by the thoughts."[2] Leonard Sweet remarks:

> Cognitive theorists tell us that you and I generate at least sixty thousand thoughts a day. That amounts to one thought every 1.44 seconds. That thought may be true or false, noble or debased, just or unjust, pure or impure, lovable or spiteful, gracious or offensive, excellent or cheap, admirable or shameful. Since every thought reverberates bio-chemically throughout the body, our thoughts shape our souls in ways we have only begun to imagine.[3]

Paul exhorts us to not conform to the pattern of the world but to be transformed by the renewing of our minds (Rom 12:2). The *New Living Translation* renders this verse as, "Let God transform you into a new person by changing the way you think." Did you know that the brain contains about two hundred billion neurons, which comprise a series of electrical highways interconnected by synapses? John Ortberg writes:

> Researchers have found that tennis players can improve their backhands simply by rehearsing them *mentally*. Neurons that will change you are firing in your mind. Over time, those pathways between neurons were shaped in ways that are absolutely unique to you. . . . Which synapses remain and which wither away depends on your mental habits. Those that carry no traffic go out of business like bus routes with no customers. Those that get

2. Wikisource, "The Thoughts of The Emperor Marcus Aurelius Antoninus," V.16.
3. Sweet, *Post-Modern Pilgrims*, 100.

heavily trafficked get stronger and thicker. The mind shapes the brain. Neurons that wire together fire together. In other words, when you practice hope, love, or joy, your mind is actually, literally, rewiring itself. Because you were made in the image of God, you have the capacity for what might be called "directed mental force."[4]

Christian theology should help us engage in *faith thinking* to inform Christian lifestyle and mission. That's the point of Colossians. What you believe influences how you behave. While Christ's crucifixion figures prominently in the Christian tradition, Christ's *resurrection*, and further, his *ascension*, figures prominently in Colossians 3. Christ now sits metaphorically at God's right hand—the place of prominence, honor, and authority. This is *Jesus is Lord* language. He rules from the limitless dwelling of heaven itself—where God is. Paul says that our ongoing practice should be to *seek* things above where Christ sits. We do that when we fixate our minds on things above where he is, not on earthly things, as a *continuous* orientation of our wills. Through our spiritual union with Christ, we are raised (spiritually resurrected) with Christ, dead to our old life, and now deeply tucked away *with Christ in God.* As a Christian, your life is secluded in the impenetrable vault of God's double locked protection—*with* Christ, *in* God.

As I write on my Mac, I'm currently on a WestJet flight from Los Angeles to Calgary. I spent a nine-day whirlwind adventure in Phoenix, Garden Grove, San Diego, Pasadena, and L.A. while I visited my aging mother in San Dimas, California. I now realize, as I try to make sense of it all, that each place was a case study in mental models at work. In Phoenix, a group of leaders from our denomination met to discuss its future in the twenty-first century. I saw a large discrepancy between some who had a corporate and control mindset and those who had a confederation and camaraderie mindset, between those whose view was management while others whose view was missional. I longed to see a magnificent surrender, where we could share our *passions* rather than state our *positions*. In Garden Grove, I taught a doctoral course on missional leadership and disciplemaking and listened to some students describe how stuck they felt in their established "attractional" churches that had little sense of mission and service to their communities. They felt out of sync with the mental models of some of their colleagues. In

---

4. Ortberg, *The Me I Want to Be*, 97–98.

San Diego, I met with a seminary dean at work on a Masters degree track in missional leadership. We got straight to the point. When our hour meeting concluded, I knew we had connected on the same wavelength. In Pasadena and Los Angeles I attended a Sunday morning and evening service of Mosaic, where Erwin McManus pastors. The speaker preached on John 11 where Jesus declared that he was the resurrection and the life and demonstrated it when he raised Lazarus from death. The narrative revolves around the scandal that Mary and Martha, the Jews, the Pharisees, Caiaphas, and the disciples experienced, as Jesus jarred their understanding about his time line and his words and works about death, sleep, and resurrection. The preacher at Mosaic helped us think theologically about our own mental models concerning death. Then, I saw raw ruin on CNN news, as I viewed actor Charlie Sheen rant about his expulsion by Warner Brothers from his sit-com *Two and a Half Men* and Libyan leader Gadhafi rant about his power.

The common theme in these examples is the importance of ingrained mental models and how we interpret and live in our earthly worlds through them. We perceive our "reality" through very limited eyes—our own. Someone said, "We don't see the world as it is, but as we are." But we must see the world through the lens of Christ as Lord. If we are raised with him, like a mystic, we must develop that mental model and daily set our minds on him. In Colossians 3:1–4, Paul invites us to cultivate a Christian worldview—one that fixates on Jesus Christ, the raised and ascended Lord who rules and in whom we live, for Christ is our life (v. 4). It's an all-encompassing Christian worldview, or mental model, that will shape our lives to embody the truths we champion. This requires deliberate concentration. In Colossians 3, Paul exhorts us to be so heavenly minded (vv. 1–4) that we become so earthly good (vv. 5–25). Our universal worldview claim must prove itself in *praxis*. Ponder the significance of this quote:

> It is the universality of a worldview's claim—its appeal to the broadest horizon of reference conceivable—that makes it applicable to all domains of life. Consequently, a worldview is only as good as the *praxis* or way of life that it engenders. That is why, in the rhetoric of this epistle, Paul's critique of the Colossian philosophy is concerned less with matters of theory and doctrine than with *praxis*. . . . The proof of the truth of the gospel that Paul proclaims is not in the power of his rhetoric against the competition but in the "fruit" that such truth bears in the community

(1:6, 10). Therefore, the apologetic of Colossians 2 is incomplete without the moral exhortation of Colossians 3. The "philosophy" will always be a plausible alternative (2:4) as long as the truth of the gospel is not manifest in the life of the community.[5]

In other words, if Christ is supreme and sufficient, our walk will match our talk, our life will match our doctrine, and Jesus our *Lord* will be Jesus our *Life*. If we died to our old life and are raised with Christ, then Christ is now our life. He lives in us. Paul affirms, "I have been crucified with Christ and I no longer live, but Christ lives in me. The life I live in the body, I live by faith in the Son of God, who loved me and gave himself for me" (Gal 2:20). Because Christ is in us, we have the hope of glory (Col 1:27). We will appear with him when he returns because we are securely secluded in him. As we accompany him our raised life will be revealed. That reality should shape how we live. If we have beliefs that are distanced from actions, we live a pretend spiritual life. Paul posits a *theo-logical* conclusion. In other words, there's a practical logic that flows from God and signalled by another *therefore*. Here's the *theo-logical* conclusion, "Put to death, *therefore*, whatever belongs to your earthly nature: sexual immorality, impurity, lust, evil desires and greed, which is idolatry. Because of these, the wrath of God is coming. You used to walk in these ways, in the life you once lived" (Col 3:5–7).

We can no longer live as we once did because we are no longer the people we once were. This is spiritual formation. Now this isn't easy. God's at work in us by his Spirit but we must also cooperate with our part. We must become what we are. Because we are raised to heaven, we must live like it on earth. We do this through Christian *counter practices* (what some refer to as spiritual disciplines or habits). The first counter practice is to *kill* the evil junk that belongs to an earthly, immoral, idolatrous life. Spirituality is *embodied*. This carries implications for how we *live* the Christian faith. As people, we are comprised of physical, emotional, intellectual, and spiritual aspects. Dallas Willard reminds us that salvation and spirituality are bodily—we live in our body, our physical house, where both the Spirit and our sin interact.[6] Elsewhere Paul writes, "If by the Spirit you put to death the misdeeds of the body you will live" (Rom 8:13).

---

5. Walsh and Keesmaat, *Colossians Remixed*, 113–14.
6. See Willard, *The Spirit of the Disciplines*.

The reality of our raised and hidden heavenly life must reveal itself in the moral and spiritual quality of our earthly life. Sexual immorality, impurity, lust, evil desires, greed, and idolatry, surface one way or another in virtually every culture throughout history. The cancer of sin that saturates the earthly nature relentlessly infects and infests the practices of immorality and idolatry. Las Vegas and Hollywood, Thailand and Japan, are modern day examples of concentrated immorality and idolatry. As Old Testament Canaanite religion revealed, immorality and idolatry were often intertwined. One seems to affect the other, as *self* is the center of both. Immorality destroys genuine love for people as one seeks *self*-satisfaction through *self*-indulgence at another's expense. Immorality (and lust) dehumanizes, degrades, and exploits other people, especially women. Idolatry destroys genuine love for God as one seeks *self*-service through greed or something other than God, at God's expense. Idolatry displaces, degrades, and dethrones the true and only holy God of the universe.

God reserved pure sexual intimacy for the covenant marriage relationship between one husband and one wife—the foundation of the human family and society. It's a spiritual relationship where they become a union of one flesh designed to be fruitful and multiply (Gen 1:28; 2:24). Sexual fidelity and purity serve as one aspect of moral and spiritual evidence from heaven, what Christians hidden in Christ are to visibly practice on earth. Jesus is Lord of our sexuality and our passions. God also reserved himself for the covenant relationship between his people and himself. Because he's the only one true Creator and Redeemer, he has exclusive claim on our lives. We are his. Spiritual fidelity and purity serve as another aspect of moral and spiritual evidence from heaven, what Christians hidden in Christ are to visibly practice on earth. Jesus is Lord of our worship and our possessions.

Following the list of sensual sins, Paul makes *greed* equal to *idolatry* (v. 5; Eph 5:5). Immorality becomes an idol if we turn to sex and self-indulgence for self-satisfaction. Greed becomes an idol if we turn to material self-indulgence for self-satisfaction. Sensual and material greed are intertwined, where sex becomes a commodity—a profession, a pursuit, bought and sold, craved and advertised—in the marketplace of our culture. It is sleazy greed. Many prominent advertisers and celebrities tend to feed insatiable appetites for lust and materialism with professions and products often connected to sexuality. Increased cases of porn rings and ponzi schemes offer seedy examples of the earthly nature at work through evil desires and greed. Sensuality drives our culture as much as consumption. Immorality and idolatry are as blatant nowadays as they were in Colossae. Lady Gaga and Wall Street are just the tip of the iceberg.

God becomes angry at such sins; his divine wrath will come like an unstoppable tsunami to judge and purge (v. 6). When we grasp the magnitude of these sins and the enormity of God's fury to be unleashed, our fear of God becomes a compelling incentive to not live this way as Christians. How should we then live? We are to decisively kill, slay, and put to death, the taproot of all that belongs to our earthly nature. Exterminate these temptations at their conception. James teaches, "Each one is tempted when, by his own evil desire, he is dragged away and enticed. Then, after desire has conceived, it gives birth to sin; and sin, when it is full-grown, gives birth to death" (Jas 1:14–15). If we starve and stave off evil desires they will expire.

An old Cherokee told his grandson:

"My son, there's a battle between two wolves inside us all. One is Evil. It is anger, jealousy, greed, resentment, inferiority, lies, and ego. The other is Good. It is joy, peace, love, hope, humility, kindness, empathy, and truth."

The boy thought for a moment, and then asked his grandfather: "Which wolf wins?"

The old Cherokee quietly replied: "The one you feed."

I grew up in a non-Christian family in Southern California and lived this list as a pagan before I gave my life to Christ. If I traffic in X-rated practices and open the door to immorality or greed, the only way I will get and stay clean is through a daily magnificent surrender to Jesus as Lord in all areas of my life. I avoid or change TV or radio channels that broadcast racy content as it occurs. I try to review the content of movies before I watch them or turn them off when they are laced with sexuality. Like Job, "I made a covenant with my eyes not to look lustfully at a girl" (Job 31:1). I refuse to mouse click my way to titillating Internet sites or let sensual advertising stimulate my emotions or imagination toward consumption. We used to teach our kids that to tolerate even a small dose of immorality or greed is like placing a small piece of poop in a chocolate brownie. The smallest piece contaminates the whole. They disagreed! I daily choose to set my heart and mind on Christ, as a mental model, and strive to reject earthly impulses and invitations. What do you need to do? Are you attracted to soap operas or steamy romance novels, *National Enquirer* or celebrity fascination, pornography, gambling, incessant shopping, hoarding, or lust for another person rather than love for your spouse? What must you do to exterminate your earthly nature on a daily basis?

RENEWED

Have you ever seen the 1966 movie *Who's Afraid of Virginia Woolf,* starring Richard Burton and Elizabeth Taylor? The thirteen Oscars nominated movie depicts a verbal warzone of marital tension between George, a college history professor, and his hard-drinking wife Martha, daughter of the college president. When a young couple, played by George Segal and Sandy Dennis, arrive for a Sunday afternoon visit, George and Martha enter a scorching exchange of what Paul commands the Colossians to rid themselves: anger, rage, malice, slander, and filthy language from their lips (Col 3:8). Paul moves from immorality and idolatry to insolence. Here's another related list of *self*-centered sins that grow like nettles in the soil of the earthly nature.

Paul continues, "Do not lie to each other, since you have taken off your old self with its practices and have put on the new self, which is being renewed in knowledge in the image of its Creator" (Col 3:9–10). *Trust* is the glue of relationships. Where anger and lying prevail, trust erodes. There's almost nothing that will damage a loving community more than unrighteous anger, slander, and deceit. Evil emotions generate evil words. Filthy language and lying have no place in our lives. What was natural with our old self before we came to Christ is completely unnatural now with our new self regenerated by the Spirit. We can disagree with our words but we must not destroy with them. Rage and malice can erupt as volcanic cauldrons of verbal weaponry when we don't practice a magnificent surrender to Jesus as Lord of our communication styles. Like the evil that spewed from Dark Lord Sauron of middle earth in the movie *Lord of the Rings*, these sins spew only from the dark old self with its earthly practices.

With similar language, the nearby Ephesians were also to exchange their old self with the new self through a renewed mental attitude, "You were taught, with regard to your former way of life, to put off your old self, which is being corrupted by its deceitful desires; to be made new in the attitude of your minds; and to put on the new self, created to be like God in true righteousness and holiness" (Eph 4:22–24). Wow, we are created to be like God!

The catalogue of sins Paul identifies in Colossians 3:5–9 are rampant in our world, and prevalent, unfortunately, even in Christians. We can have so many unformed areas that we don't know where to start, especially if we are new believers. As Carlson and Lueken teach in their book *Renovation of the Church*, we can succumb to generalities, which are a good hiding place. We can acknowledge sin in our lives, but what about my lust, my temper, my ambition, my greed, my selfishness, or my words? Spiritual formation will only occur when we identify and then develop *counter practices*. In Colossians and elsewhere (cf. Gal 5:19–21; Eph 4:25–31), Paul addresses *specific* unattractive details rather than generalities, which need spiritual formation.

> As we start considering the details of our lives that need transformation, we begin seeing how automatic our responses are. We don't have to try very hard to get angry at the driver who cuts us off. Our anger comes easily and routinely because of our many years of training in it. When the circumstances arise, . . . "do the opposite of what you want to do or feel like doing." The controlling person has to put themselves in situations where someone else calls the shots. The self-absorbed person has to shut their pie hole and listen. The isolated loner needs relationships. The socialite needs solitude. The person drowning in shame needs to show up. The angry person needs to underreact. Perhaps this sounds like spiritual formation by trying hard to be different. It's actually a discipline to help us retrain our whole being in the way of Christ.[7]

While I don't want to overdramatize Paul's list of sins in Christian circles, I can honestly say that I've experienced numerous church and denominational meetings where anger, malice, and subtle slander occurred. I've seen and also heard of obstinate Christian people who've vented their pent up frustration and anger only to leave devastating results while being dismissive of others. Unfortunately, I'm guilty of the charge on more than one occasion myself where things, especially in my family life, pushed my buttons. It might seem justified for someone to "get it off their chest" rather than exercise self-control. But those on

---

7. Carlson and Lueken, *Renovation of the Church*, 123–24.

the receiving end usually have a different perspective as they suffer the destructive consequences. I've encountered angry and malicious church leaders and boards who excused their behavior with, "This is the way it is so just accept it." In other words, "This is how we operate, so get used to it. We're not open to holiness and seeking things above. We prefer practices from our old self!"

But I really like to get rid of stuff, don't you? Maybe you have a basement or garage full of junk that you want to get rid of. I love it when I can cram a pickup truck full of junk and haul it off to the dump! We use the exclamation "good riddance!" when we're glad something or someone is on their way permanently. We must rid ourselves of self-centered and self-motivated anger and slander. Scripture offers an alternative mental model and practices through love and humility—graciously talk through our differences and seek to place the interests of others above our own. Ponder this key statement, "You have taken off your old self with its practices and have put on the new self, which is being renewed in knowledge in the image of its Creator."

In the 2001 blockbuster movie *The Princess Diaries*, Anne Hathaway plays Mia, a socially awkward fifteen year-old who discovers that she's the princess of a small European country because of the recent death of her long-absent father, who, unknown to her, was the crown prince of Genovia. She must make a choice to continue the life of a San Francisco teen or step up to a life of royalty as the next in line to the throne. Mia is persuaded to have a makeover and take princess lessons from her grandmother, Queen Clarisse, played by Julie Andrews. As Mia discovers her true identity, she experiences transformation as she rises to the occasion. In effect, she is fashioned into a new image with a new appearance and new behaviors. She had to become what she was, which meant she had to discard her old life and put on her new life.

In the same way, as a chosen people who belong to God, we are a royal priesthood (1 Pet 2:9). That is our status and role. We must now experience a makeover and learn how to live like royalty. We must become what we are, and take off the shabby clothes of our old self in Adam and death and put on the designer clothes of our new self in Christ and life. Just as Jesus commanded the grave garments to be removed from Lazarus (John 11:44), so we should remove the grave garments of our old life. This transports us into a new realm where God is at work to create a new humanity (Eph 2:15) as we clothe ourselves with Christ himself (Gal 3:27; Rom 13:14). As we'll see in the next chapter, we must put on "Christian clothing" through specific practices that correspond to our new life. A magnificent surrender means that we'll work out in daily life our status and role as royalty, as we experience a makeover into God's image and take biblical lessons on how to behave like royalty! Johann Wolfgang van Goethe (1749–1832) remarked, "Behavior is the mirror in which everyone shows their image."[8]

How does this transformation of image occur? It occurs over time, progressively, in our increasing *knowledge* of God according to his image. God's Spirit transforms us from the inside out, "Therefore we do not lose heart. Though outwardly we are wasting away, yet inwardly we are being renewed day by day" (2 Cor 4:16). Children often look and act like their parents because they reflect their image. God's original intent was for human beings to reflect his image (Gen 1:26–27). Because sin permanently marred that image, Christ now displays the pattern for how a perfect human being looks and acts as a pristine icon of God. Jesus is the image (icon) of God (Col 1:15) and we are to become duplicate copies of him as God conforms us to the image of his Son (Rom 8:29). How's your image? The goal and process for our new life is personal and corporate renewal literally *into* our *full knowledge* of God, which connects us to his image.

When I was a brand new Bible college student many moons ago, two basic texts we all read were J. I. Packer, *Knowing God* and J. B. Phillips, *Your God is Too Small*. Students still need to read them. To know God is the purpose of life. Eternal life itself is that we would know the only true God and Jesus Christ whom he sent (John 17:3). John Calvin, who wrote *Institutes of the Christian Religion*, begins his theological masterpiece in Book 1 with an exposition of "The Knowledge of God the Creator." Nothing is more important than that we are renewed in our knowledge of God. A distorted knowledge of God leads to a distorted life. Our knowledge of God must correspond as exactly as possible to who God truly is as revealed in Jesus, for God is "Jesus-like!" Jesus taught, "Anyone who has seen me has seen the Father" (John 14:9).

God chose knowledge to shape our understanding of him that will begin to transform us into his image by the Spirit. As we increase in our full knowledge of him, we begin to look more like him in our character and conduct. This is the goal of Christian theology. Memorize this text:

8. Goethe and Boyesen, *Goethe's Works*, 319.

"His divine power has given us everything we need for life and godliness through our knowledge of him who called us by his own glory and goodness" (2 Pet 1:3). Read Scripture, pay attention to the creation, observe how God is reflected in others, and pay attention to the ways in which God is at work in the world around you. When you do, you will acquire a renewing of your knowledge of God that makes you more like him.

There's lots of talk these days about church and denominational renewal. While there's a place for structural renewal and certainly spiritual renewal (see Tit 3:5), we need a renewal of a full knowledge of God—*theological* renewal—and the renewing of our minds (Rom 12:2) for transformation to occur in our lives and churches. This results in a *new humanity*—one new family—where there's no social, ethnic, or economic divisions between people, because Christ is all, and is in all (Col 3:11; cf. Gal 3:27–28). Our union with Christ creates spiritual solidarity with others. Paul's absolute theological statement that "Christ is all, and is in all," widens our mental models. Eric Porterfield summarizes it this way,

> Only someone through whom *all* things were created, someone who holds *all* things together, and someone who reconciles *all* things to God can bring *all* people together. Because Christ is "in *all*" of his followers, they are one in him, regardless of who they are, where they are from, or what they look like.[9]

What's Paul's main idea for us to personalize in Colossians 3:1–11? Let me suggest it's this: *become so heavenly minded that you are so earthly good*. How? Daily set your heart and mind skyward where Christ sits. Then kill and put off your old earthly self with its practices, while you put on your new self being renewed into God's image in Christ. This is a life-long journey of spiritual formation, where God renews us in knowledge according to his image while we choose to practice a magnificent surrender to Christ who is all and in all. This leaves little room for immorality, idolatry, anger, slander, and deceit, because Christ is our life. For a parallel reflection, notice Paul's instructions to the nearby church at Ephesus:

> Be imitators of God, therefore, as dearly loved children and live a life of love, just as Christ loved us and gave himself up for us as a fragrant offering and sacrifice to God. But among you there

9. Porterfield, *Sessions with Colossians and Philemon*, 68 (italics in the original).

must not be even a hint of sexual immorality, or of any kind of impurity, or of greed, because these are improper for God's holy people. Nor should there be obscenity, foolish talk or coarse joking, which are out of place, but rather thanksgiving. For of this you can be sure: No immoral, impure or greedy person—such a man is an idolater—has any inheritance in the kingdom of Christ and of God. (Eph 5:1–5)

Let me offer yet another Scottish church leader whose devotional depth might inspire your prayer. Dr. John Baillie (1886–1960), a Church of Scotland minister, was Professor of divinity at the University of Edinburgh from 1934 to 1956. In 1914, after his brother Peter drowned while training to serve as a missionary in India and two close friends died in World War I, Baillie volunteered to serve with the YMCA among British soldiers in France. After the war he became chair of Christian theology at Auburn Theological Seminary, New York, and then taught at Emmanuel College, Toronto before he became Roosevelt Professor of Systematic Theology at Union Seminary, New York. His book, *Our Knowledge of God* (1939), regarded by many as his best, explored the relationship between the knowledge of God and spiritual and moral experience. After he retired in 1957 from New College, Edinburgh, he was named a Companion of Honor to Queen Elizabeth II. Baillie also wrote a devotional classic, *A Diary of Private Prayer* (1936). What follows is one of his prayers that you might personalize:

O Thou to whom I owe the gift of this day's life, give to me also, I beseech Thee, the spirit to use it as I ought. Forbid that I should stain the brightness of the morning with any evil thought or darken the noontide with any shameful deed. Let Thy Holy Spirit breathe into my heart today all pure and heavenly desires. Let Thy truth inform my mind. Let Thy justice and righteousness make a throne within me and rule my errant will. Let Christ be formed in me, and let me learn of Him all lowliness of heart, all gentleness of bearing, all modesty of speech, all helpfulness of action, and promptness in the doing of my Father's will. Amen.[10]

REFLECTION FOR GROUPS AND INDIVIDUALS

1. Read Colossians 3:1–4 in several translations and consult a few commentaries. Seek to paraphrase it and draw out the meaning of

10. Baillie, *A Diary of Private Prayer*, 109.

the deep truths contained in this hinge text. Reflect as a group or as an individual on how this text relates to what precedes and now serves to move to what follows and the significance of our mental models in our perceptions and lives.

2. Carefully read and analyze the quote by Walsh and Keesmaat. What is the central point they are making? What is *praxis* and how does it relate to a Christian worldview claim? How does this apply to you as a group or as an individual?

3. Discuss Colossians 3:5–9 and how immorality and idolatry are related, and how anger, lust, and lying come from practices of the earthly nature (your old self; your life before you came to Christ). Evaluate the extent to which you experience personally or corporately any of these *specific* sins. How will you root them out of your life through *counter practices*? What does it mean for you to put on your new self being renewed in the knowledge of the image of God and how do you do that as a group or as an individual?

PRACTICE FOR GROUPS AND INDIVIDUALS

1. As a group or individual, memorize Colossians 3:1–4. Rehearse it daily, to set the framework for your mental model and concentration. Develop a mental discipline that is "heavenly minded" to be "earthly good." Imagine Christ as your life, living in you and through you, where both your salvation and spirituality are housed and expressed *bodily*.

2. Daily monitor your emotions and your temptations and become aware of the extent to which they are stimulated by or toward sensuality or consumerism. Determine to kill earthly practices at their conception and rid yourself of them, as you would junk. Guard your eyes, ears, and emotions when confronted with advertising, music, movies, TV, Internet, and other forms of popular media culture that traffic in immorality and consumerism. Do not permit anger, slander, malice, or lying to ever take place in your life as a group or as an individual.

3. Purchase a copy of John Baillie's, *A Diary of Private Prayer*, and pray through his daily prayers for thirty-one days, in your group and/or individual settings.

6

Christian Clothing

"Spiritual formation, good or bad, is always profoundly social. You cannot keep it to yourself. Anyone who says, 'It's just between me and God' has misunderstood God as well as 'me.' For all that is between me and God affects who I am; and that, in turn, modifies my relationship to everyone around me. My relationship to others also modifies me and deeply affects my relationship to God. Hence those relationships must be transformed if I am to be transformed."[1]

THE CLOTHING INDUSTRY IS a multi-billion dollar industry. Supermodels and fashion capture people's imaginations. Advertisers hire celebrities to pitch their products as fashion trendsetters. The media also pays lively attention to what celebrities wear in public and in private—whether it's Jennifer Aniston at the Oscars or Kate Middleton in the outdoors. Most malls are packed with clothing and shoe stores whose well-dressed mannequins tempt you to move beyond mere window-shopping and inside for a storewide sale. Magazine racks and supermarket cashier aisles are congested with well-placed magazines whose covers are designed to entice us with beauty and appearance. Nevertheless, someone remarked, "Fashion is the science of appearances, and it inspires one with the desire to seem rather than to be." Conventional wisdom retorts, "It's not what you wear but who you are that matters." And that's where Paul leads us next:

---

1. Willard, *Renovation of the Heart*, 182.

> Therefore, as God's chosen people, holy and dearly loved, clothe yourselves with compassion, kindness, humility, gentleness and patience. Bear with each other and forgive whatever grievances you may have against one another. Forgive as the Lord forgave you. And over all these virtues put on love, which binds them all together in perfect unity. (Col 3:12–14)

Paul applies the Old Testament imagery of Israel as God's chosen, holy, and loved people (e.g. Deut 7:6–8), to the Colossians. These are terms of election and endearment. The church is the new humanity as the new Israel. God selects a new wardrobe that we as new people should wear—Christian clothes! Imagine the warmth and charm of compassion, kindness, humility, gentleness and patience. These five dazzling virtues are glorious garments that we must put on in contrast to the dark vices we were supposed to have taken off (Col 3:8–9).

ALL YOU NEED IS LOVE

Did you read the quote at the beginning by Dallas Willard? That summarizes the main point of what spiritual formation includes—*relationships*—love for God and people. In many ways *our* spiritual formation is *for the sake of other people* in how we treat them. We practice Christian faith in community not in isolation. There's a crucial place for solitude and a personal devotional life, but we must then re-emerge into daily life where we publicly live out our faith. When we embrace a magnificent surrender to Christ Jesus as Lord, we live in him in the context of relationships. And that's because God as Trinity is relational and social.

The incentive for spiritual formation both individually and corporately is *theological*, as we are God's chosen people, holy and dearly loved. We are elected, set apart, and loved by Him. We did not choose him but he chose us before the foundation of the world in Jesus Christ (Eph 1:4). Because God loves us, that secure place of election and endearment empowers us to love others (1 John 4:11). We can focus our attention on the so-called *spiritual* disciplines such as Bible study and prayer, solitude and submission, worship and service. But we must always connect these to the *relational* disciplines of compassion, kindness, humility, gentleness, and patience. These five virtues will strikingly adorn our lives as we continually clothe ourselves with them by actual practice in community. This requires focused intention and discipline.

I've had to "eat crow" more times than I can recall. I can be insensitive and I can let my type A personality get the worst of me. I can sweat the small stuff or make issues based on principle. Over the years, I've made issues with my wife, my kids, and other leaders, and have had to come back and apologize for my words or attitudes, often with tears and deep remorse. I understand how difficult it is to change and to practice especially humility, gentleness, and patience—and they all partner together. I know it takes boundless composure to tolerate controlling, rude, or antagonistic people. But I must *practice* these five virtues.

Andrew Murray wrote, "Humility is the bloom and beauty of holiness. The chief mark of counterfeit holiness is its lack of humility. . . . The holiest will be the humblest."[2] What if, just as Jesus did, we practiced humility as an *attitude* (Phil 2:5)? Do you think it would cultivate more gentleness and patience in us with people, leading us to also "bear with each other and forgive whatever grievances you may have against one another" (Col 3:13)? Do you have a *grievance* with someone? What would it take for you to forgive them and let it go? Mentioned twice in this verse, *forgiveness* makes true Christian community possible. Again, there's a theological motivation for this relational discipline, "Forgive as the Lord forgave you."

Like draping ourselves in a twenty-five hundred dollar sheepskin leather coat to cover all that we wear, "over all these virtues we are to put on love, which binds them all together in perfect unity" (v. 14). The Beatles sang, "All you need is love." Love blankets and choreographs these five virtues in perfect unity. Douglas Moo observes, "Compassion, kindness, humility, gentleness, and patience attain their full power only when they are unified by and empowered by love . . . and it is the 'new self,' the community, that will be brought to perfection when love binds the virtues together."[3] Why do we tend to think that current techniques and models will grow a church and cultivate church health? Why do we tend to focus on church leadership development? Is the Christian movement based on leadership techniques? Donald Miller blogs:

> I am reminded the movement we are in is, first and foremost, a movement of *love*. And I am reminded that love is a force, the most powerful of forces. We shouldn't think of it in weak terms any longer. How insufficient a choice is it, then, to replace love

2. Murray, *Humility*, 62, 65.

3. Moo, *The Letter to the Colossians and to Philemon*, 282.

with leadership techniques, which so often amount to worldly manipulation?[4]

What if you knew that you only had one week left to live? Would you want to argue, have issues, hold resentment, raise your voice, or express any disdain for others? I bet you'd want to be gentle, patient, forgiving, and loving toward a partner, a sibling, a child, a boss, a pastor, or others at church. When we take people and life for granted, we forget that life is short. We focus on the negative, sweat the small stuff, and lose sight of what really matters. At our funeral will we be remembered for how much we loved or for how much we languished? Robert Browning mused, "Take away love and our earth is a tomb."[5] Servant leadership, which should really be *love* leadership, is hollow if it's merely a style rather than the substance. Love is patient and kind, is not rude, self-seeking, or easily angered, and keeps no record of wrongs (1 Cor 13:4–5). Love believes the best. Plato taught, "At the touch of love everyone becomes a poet."

As a district executive coach, I consult with many leaders and churches. I've seen that most church leaders, staffs, and boards need to develop better organizational leadership skills. Most of them also need to become more outward focused and missional. What I find amazing and discouraging, though, is how many churches suffer from internal relational tension. One of our churches was known in the community as, "Oh, that's the church that fights!" We also have churches that "splant-ed" other churches. This is where a dissenting group of people cause a church split and leave to plant another church while they also carry their relational tension and baggage with them. This new church split/plant effectively becomes a church "splant." In a seminar I heard Hugh Halter say, "Whatever is not transformed is transmitted." With the mounds of Bible study, prayer, worship, and sermons that Christians are exposed to you'd think that our levels of holiness and humility would be stellar. However, mere exposure to information and even encounters with God do not automatically translate into transformation. It takes *practice*.

We must practice letting the peace of Christ rule (like an umpire) in our hearts, "since as members of one body we were called to peace and not discord, and to be thankful" (Col 3:15). The problem is that

4. Donald Miller, "How Christ Built an Army Without Weapons," *Donald Miller* (blog), April 18, 2011, http://donmilleris.com/2011/04/18/getting-behind-the-movement-of -christ/.

5. Brooke, *The Poetry of Robert Browning*, 224.

we function as our own self-appointed umpire who judges the plays while we veto Christ's rule. We don't engage in magnificent surrender and live in Christ Jesus as *Lord*. Paul also commanded similar practices for the Ephesians about one hundred twenty miles away, "Be completely humble and gentle; be patient, bearing with one another in love. Make every effort to keep the unity of the Spirit through the bond of peace" (Eph 4:2–3). This sounds like a duplicate copy of Colossians 3:12–15. These believers had similar problems then as we do today: pride, impatience, hardness, intolerance, and ingratitude fostered animosity. But when we die to self-interest and personal agendas, and are thankful, we let Christ's peace umpire our disputes.

In addition, we must "let the word of Christ dwell in you richly as you teach and admonish one another with all wisdom, and as you sing psalms, hymns and spiritual songs with gratitude in your hearts to God" (Col 3:16). Wow, when we gather as a corporate body of Christians, we must permit the word about Christ to live among us richly as it fosters Christian spiritual and social formation. We can study, teach, and know the word, but the command is to allow this word to take up residence in our lives. If we are to release the riches of living in the Lord, this will only occur when this living word actually lives among his people. *Christology* is the curriculum for church life. Furthermore, the indwelling word leads to inspiring wisdom and worship that flow through mutual teaching, singing, and gratitude in our hearts to God. Can you sense the ethos, the feeling, and the atmosphere of these commands? Does your heart long to experience this quality of Christian life and church experience? What will it take to get it there?

Now let your imagination soar. Dream the highest motto or the widest slogan that could direct a purpose-driven life. I remember when I was a Boy Scout our motto was, "Be prepared." I also remember our slogan was, "Do a good deed daily." The Boy Scouts was a great training ground in character and skill development for me as a young boy. I earned enough merit badges to become a Star scout but never made it to Life or Eagle. Over time, I lost interest and left the Scouts. The motto and slogan are good. We may have our own personal or professional mottos or slogans like "Get ahead," or "Practice the golden rule," or "Think different," or "Just do it."

But Paul offers a motto whose comprehensive finality invites a magnificent surrender as stunning and decisive as a game-winning goal in a

World Cup soccer match. He draws together all he wrote since the first bookend in Colossians 2:6, "So then, just as you received Christ Jesus as Lord, continue to live (your life) in him." He then offers the second bookend as a concluding motto, "And whatever you do, whether in word or deed, do it all in the name of the Lord Jesus, giving thanks to God the Father through him" (Col 3:17). Notice, *whatever you do*—talking or training, shopping or serving, parenting or performing, walking or waiting. *We are what we repeatedly do.* This covers it all when it's *in the name of*—representing the reality and character of—the *Lord* Jesus. So here's a good reality check: whatever you say or do, would you want Christ's name pinned to it? Finally, notice how God-focused thanksgiving appears again as a key spiritual practice in Colossians. Our lives are to be an anthem of praise and thanksgiving to God.

The call to a total life lived in the Lord is both audacious and unimaginable! What church can say, "We live like this?" But this is theological life, informed and shaped by the sublime *reality* of Jesus Christ the risen and ascended *Lord.* Picture him seated as King in heaven! Should we not resolve to daily practice such resplendent surrender? I feel compelled to do a rigorous spiritual inventory of my character and develop a *rule of life* that emblazons this motto over it.

As I write, Easter Sunday is three days away. My friend Len posted this reflection on *Facebook*: "This Sunday I speak on the resurrection, and it's my first time speaking on Easter Sunday. I am excited, terrified, and depressed—all at the same time. Resurrection, among Christians, is often just another doctrine, another point in a belief system. Who is adequate for these things? I can't help feeling that if anyone leaves Sunday morning thinking 'ho-hum, another Easter done' I have failed." Here was my reply on his wall: "Easter's great. But that's an incomplete story if you don't also include the *ascension*. He is risen but also reigning from heaven with the practical implications of that (Eph 1:20–23; 4:7–10; Col 3:1–4; Rom 8:24; etc.)." We are also seated with him there (Eph 2:6; Col 3:1)! Dear reader, because Jesus is risen indeed, *and* ascended, he's Lord—the summit of New Testament theology. What Paul stated in 2:6 now comes full circle in 3:17, "Whatever you do, whether in word or deed, do it all in the name of the Lord Jesus, giving thanks to God the Father through him!"

CHRISTIAN HOUSEHOLDS

A magnificent surrender to the Lord Jesus will permeate and shape our speech and conduct in every segment of our lives. Living in him will release subterranean riches that simultaneously transcend and yet work within the very structure of our society and our families. Paul now applies his "whatever you do" statement above to Christian households. We could reason, if our Christian faith isn't working at home, then it isn't working. He addresses how *Christian* relationships are to function between wives and husbands, children and parents, fathers and children, and slaves and masters, who are *Christians* (Col 3:18—4:1). His teaching is similar to that in Ephesians 5:22—6:9. There's evidence that *household codes* developed in Greco-Roman and Stoic settings inherited from Aristotle, parallel the structure contained in Colossians. They stress a hierarchy of husband over wife, father over children, and master over slaves.

Under Roman law, women, children, and slaves, were considered legal property, with few rights or privileges. Men and masters ruled the roost! Today's rightful emphasis on women's rights, children and families at risk, and labor laws, were simply non-existent in the ancient world. Paul does not defend Roman law nor does he endorse male domination over women and children nor slavery. Love, and not law, must prevail. Though Paul instructs wives to *submit* to their husbands, children to *obey* their parents, and slaves to *obey* their masters, the framework is *in the Lord*. It is notable that he addresses those in the subservient role (wives, children, slaves) before he addresses those in the superior role (husbands, parents, masters).

He Christianizes and thus revolutionizes the responsibilities of households as he considers each member as *people*. He places both duties and rights on all of them, but lays the weight of responsibility on those in a stronger position—men and masters! The divine pattern transcends the domination and oppression perpetrated by pagan culture. The resulting transformation, however, is *subversive*. It works from within, from an ethic of what William Barclay calls *reciprocal obligation*. He writes, "It is never an ethic on which all the duties are on one side. As Paul saw it, husbands have as great an obligation as wives; parents have just as binding a duty as children; masters have their responsibilities as much as slaves."[6]

Paul does not eliminate the hierarchical structure or the social or gender distinctions between men and women, husbands and wives, parents and children, and masters and slaves. He does not directly argue for *social equality* per sé. Yes, many point to Galatians 3:28, "There is neither Jew nor Greek, slave nor free, male nor female, for you are all one in Christ Jesus." But in the context of Galatians 3, Paul does not eradicate social or gender distinctions. Rather, he establishes a theological and spiritual equality of identity, dignity, and privilege based on the promise to Abraham and not the law, which supersedes social or gender status. His bookends around verse 28 are, "You are all sons of God through faith in Christ Jesus . . . If you belong to Christ, then you are Abraham's seed, and heirs according to promise" (Gal 3:26, 29). In other words, there is no pecking order, no lower position on the totem pole, and no next in line to the throne for those who put their faith in Christ.

It is possible Paul offered a *subversive* counter theological point to the daily morning prayer of orthodox Jewish men that indicated basic distinctions in ancient society where they thanked God that they were not made a Gentile, a slave, or a woman. All become equal family members and equal heirs in him—men and women, religious and non-religious, privileged and outcast, alike. This is *subversive* counter-cultural good news—the gospel—especially for the marginalized: slaves, women, children, and Gentiles! Colossians shows that as a first principle, submission to the Lord as head of the church is incumbent on every Christian in the household.

It's interesting that Paul began with *wives*. Why? Perhaps it was because of their low status in the ancient world but also because of their high significance in the home. They are to *submit* to their husbands as is "fitting in the Lord" (3:18). This doesn't mean they'll place themselves under unquestioning servitude to a domineering or abusive husband. It also doesn't mean they'll become militant liberationists out to overthrow the tyranny of men or become subservient but *Desperate Housewives* embroiled in secrets and scandals. Rather, it means, with voluntary willingness they will rank themselves under their husband's role as their head, as Christ is head of his church (see Eph 5:23). Wives are to submit to their husbands as the church submits to Christ (Eph 5:24). This implies

6. Barclay, *The Letters to the Philippians, Colossians, and Thessalonians*, 160–61.

alignment not subjection. The relationship in the Christian household is spiritual. Wives are usually willing to follow a *loving* husband.

Paul then instructs husbands to "*love* your wives and not be harsh with them" (3:19). The standard is actually higher for the guys and revolutionary, as no household codes of the day contained this duty. This kind of love is not romantic or erotic love but *agape* love—the sacrificial and self-giving love that is patterned after Christ's love for the church (Eph 5:25). It means that the husband as head of the wife is head lover not head manager over the household. Again, men should put on the Christian clothing of love (3:14). When they do, they will then not be harsh or bitter with their wives. Husbands seem to have a propensity for being harsh and demanding. The *macho man* is not Christian. Infidelity, wife beating, spousal abuse, and divorce are rampant in our society. Though not exclusively, husbands are often the key perpetrators. Someone remarked, "The main cause of divorce is marriage!" In our culture women are also often exploited as sexual objects. Movies, television, music videos, and advertising ceaselessly shape our culture with this. Christian husbands must not become couch potatoes devoted only to their work and to their sports and hang out only with their buddies, while they ignore their wife's needs and expect them to gratify the husband's. Husbands must take their cues from Christ.

In addition, Paul instructs, "Fathers, do not embitter your children, or they will become discouraged" (3:21). Fathers seem to also have a propensity for being harsh with their children. In the ancient world, fathers were responsible to command their children. Many people today (me included), say that their father was too commanding and stern, too strict and critical, that they could never please him, nor saw proof that he loved them. John Newton remarked, "I know that my father loved me—but he did not seem to wish me to see it."[7] The father with a misguided though well-intentioned motive to correct, discipline, and push their children into being responsible, can overdo it and provoke discouragement, resentment, and rebellion. They can cause children to lose heart or despise themselves. There's a delicate balance of loving correction that's firm yet flexible. I believe that a slap on the back usually works better than a kick in the rear! When we note the backgrounds of chronic criminals, sexual abusers, pedophiles, and rioters, we often discover that they had abusive, violent, or demanding fathers and dysfunctional fam-

7. As cited by Barclay, ibid., 163.

ily systems. The principle of *father power* is this: as the father goes, often go the children.

However, on the other side of the equation, Paul also directs his instruction to the kids, "Children, *obey* your parents in everything, for this pleases the Lord" (3:20). This is rather comprehensive, as children are to obey (listen under) their parents *in everything*. Children tend to want to live with total freedom without responsibility. Resistance to their parent's authority starts early on when they are toddlers and often emerges full bloom in the teen years. Yet Christian children have a responsibility to submit to the authority of their parents while they live under their roof and also to the Lord, as this pleases him. Again, this shapes the spiritual alignment of the roles and responsibilities in Christian households. For this to work, each family member must be accountable to the Lord. Through obedience, children begin to learn submission, and eventually a magnificent surrender, which forms the basis of Christian spiritual formation through living in the Lord. This new humanity lived out in this family system offers untold treasures and rewards. Proper self-image, joy, and purpose in life are formed in the womb of Christian family life where parents and children alike have *reciprocal obligations*.

As I write, I've been married thirty-two years to my dear wife Gail. We have one daughter and two sons. Marriage and family forms the basis of society, but they have fallen on hard times in our culture with pre-nuptial agreements and open fire on children's moral instruction. I evaluate my marriage and role as a husband and father and feel the gnawing regret where I wish I did some things very differently. There are times when I was harsh with both my wife and children, where out of frustration or anger I said or did things that wounded or embittered them. I've read and listened to material by *Focus on the Family*, Barbara Coloroso, and even Dr. Phil. I've studied the pros and cons of the exegetical and practical arguments between *egalitarians* and *complementarians* regarding the biblical role of women and men.[8] I've tried to love my wife and not exasperate my children. I'm not as bad as I could be or as some others are, but I'm not as good as I should be either. I can blame it on my upbringing in a pagan family of twice divorced parents, devoid of consistent affirmation, love, and affection. But my parents grew

---

8. For resources and discussions for both sides of the issue see: *Christians for Biblical Equality*: http://www.cbeinternational.org/; and *The Council on Biblical Manhood & Womanhood*: http://www.cbmw.org/.

up in dysfunctional and broken families too. Bad habits and personal hurts are deeply ingrained. I take responsibility. Christian marriage and family counseling should establish its goal and substance in theological and spiritual terms more than in psychological terms. Paul's instructions to Christian households in Colossae are concerned with the spiritual formation and discipleship of all its members, as each one learns to live in the Lord in magnificent surrender to him—men, women, children, slaves, and masters.

There are two redeeming factors in my spiritual journey. One is that my wife is a five-star example of an impeccable, though imperfect, wife who willingly submits to her husband as is fitting in the Lord—even when I fail at times to love her as Christ loves the church and have been harsh with her at times. In many ways, her model of what it looks like to be a noble wife and mother inspires and instructs me in what it looks like to be a better husband and father. She loves and cares deeply, and embodies a deep respect for people. The other factor is the grace of God ceaselessly at work in my life. As I continue to draw from the deep, bubbling, artesian well of God's untiring offer of second chances, I can drink from the invigorating fullness that I have in Christ. Somehow, as I practice repeated repentance with godly sorrow, ask for forgiveness, eat crow, and start fresh, the Word and Spirit inform and enliven my family experience. I'm still learning how to love my wife and children in the Lord. I'm learning to leave my regrets behind, and embrace Joan Chittister's words for the present,

> The burden of regret is that, unless we come to understand the value of the choices we made in the past, we may fail to see the gifts they have brought us.

> The blessing of regret is clear—it brings us, if we are willing to face it head on, to the point of being present to this new time of life in an entirely new way. It urges us on to continue becoming.[9]

And now Paul tackles one of the greatest social dilemmas of all time—the relationship between slaves and masters (3:22—4:1). One can recount savage slavery that thrived in Great Britain, the United States, and the Sudan, in South Asia as debt slaves, and depicted in the television series based on Alex Haley's book *Roots*. Paul proportionately devotes more space to this section than to the previous, and likely for

---

9. Chittister, *The Gift of Years*, 5 (italics in the original).

good reason. Estimates are that there were about sixty million slaves in the Roman Empire, where it was beneath the dignity of a Roman citizen to work.[10] Slaves did practically all of the work. However, there were vast differences between the modern institution of slavery and those in the ancient world. Wayne Grudem explains,

> [There were] differences between the horrible institution of slavery as it was practiced in America before the mid-nineteenth century and the first-century institution described by the Greek term *doulos* (the Greek word which is usually translated "slave" or "servant" in the New Testament, but which the NASB and NKJV often better translate as "bond-servant" or "bondservant," showing that it was a different institution) . . . this was the most common employment situation in the Roman Empire in the time of the New Testament. A bondservant could not quit his job or seek another employer until he obtained his freedom, but there were extensive laws that regulated the treatment of such bondservants and gave them considerable protection. Bondservants could own their own property and often purchased their freedom by about age thirty, and they often held positions of significant responsibility such as teachers, physicians, nurses, managers of estates, retail merchants, and business executives. . . . This helps to understand why the New Testament did not immediately prohibit the institution of "bondservants," while at the same time giving principles that led to its eventual prohibition.[11]

Imagine all the Christian slaves and masters present from the households gathered that day to hear a letter read that Paul wrote to the Colossians as well as to those in Laodicea. Douglas Moo comments, "The ancient household was often far larger than our typical 'nuclear' family, including not just parents and their young children, but older children (and sometimes their spouses) as well as domestic slaves."[12] I wonder what it was like for all these people to hear this, perhaps for the first time, in a public setting. Paul's letter would captivate their attention when they heard his cultural references. There's power in publicly read Scripture.

10. Barclay, *The Letters to the Galatians and Ephesians*, 179.

11. Grudem, *Evangelical Feminism*, 78–79. Also see Grudem, *Evangelical Feminism and Biblical Truth*, 339–45.

12. Moo, ibid., 308.

Just as children were to obey their parents in everything, slaves were to also obey their *earthly* masters in everything (3:22). They were to obey, not simply when their master's eye was on them, nor to superficially win their favor. Literally, they were not to engage in "eye-service" as *people-pleasers*. They were to work as hard for their boss, in reality rather than in appearance, whether or not he was looking at them. Slaves were to obey their masters with sincerity (singleness) of heart and reverence (fear) for the Lord. The fear of God is a prominent phrase in Scripture. It denotes the awe and submission we offer to God. R. Kent Hughes remarked, "The pagan slave served his master because he was bound by fear; the Christian slaved served his master *better* because he feared God. Working hard at our tasks from the heart brings glory to God."[13] Paul goes further, "Whatever you do, work at it with all your heart, as working for the Lord, not for men" (3:23). The Lord expects single-hearted and full-hearted work that any slave would actually do for him were he their earthly master. This would be a tough challenge for slaves whose work was a hardship.

But notice an eschatological reason, "Since you know that you will receive an inheritance from the Lord as a reward. It is the Lord Christ you are serving" (3:24). This refers to *the* inheritance of the kingdom of God and salvation in the age to come, where true liberation and freedom will be an experience for all believers. A slave would have little hope of inheriting anything. Perhaps this is also a *subversive* reference to the inheritance they now receive according to the liberation they now experience, for in Christ they also "share in the inheritance of the saints in the kingdom of light. For he has rescued us from the dominion of darkness and brought us into the kingdom of the Son he loves, in whom we have redemption" (Col 1:12–13). Therefore, they should work as freedmen with an inheritance. This is a true liberation theology, which concerns itself with the poor, the outcast, the oppressed, and the slave—not as a static doctrinaire political cause, but as a dynamic faith-as-trust in Christ Jesus as Lord movement empowered by the reign of God's justice.[14]

This is a Christian work ethic that transcends whatever cultural work situation in which we find ourselves. Christian slaves would have to approach obedience to their masters from a theological rather than from an economic or personal motivation and enthusiasm. In addition,

13. Hughes, *Colossians and Philemon*, 131 (italics in the original).
14. See Harvey Cox, *The Future of Faith*.

they could rest confident in God's fair justice and impartiality where Paul taught, "Anyone who does wrong will be repaid for his wrong, and there is no favoritism" (3:25). His final brief exhortation places an obligation on masters to be right and fair with their slaves, "Masters (lords), provide your slaves with what is right and fair, because you know that you also have a Master (Lord) in heaven" (4:1). These words are revolutionary in a society that denied justice and fairness to slaves. Again, the motivation for a master to treat his slaves with dignity and fairness is *theological*. No matter how high a mountain of social status we climb, God will always be the king of the mountain. Earthly lords have a heavenly Lord that holds them to a higher ethical standard. Jesus Christ expects a magnificent surrender from Christian wives, husbands, children, slaves, *and masters*. As they surrender to him as Lord, they will transcend and transform the structures and systems of any oppressive aspects of culture from the inside out. Consult the parallel passage in Ephesians 6:5–9. How do Paul's instructions addressed to slaves and masters *then*, however, speak to us *today*?

This poses a challenge in *hermeneutics*—the process of interpretation and application of Scripture. We don't live in a culture like those of the ancient world where slavery was practiced. We aren't slaves; we don't own slaves; and slavery is illegal in every country of the world, (though it is still practiced in some places). How do we apply what Paul wrote to a specific cultural context then to our context today as God's *living word*? Are we to apply the household codes by obeying our bosses and work for them as for the Lord? Are bosses obligated to treat their employees fairly because they have a boss in heaven? Do we apply *principles* that we uncover regarding the dignity of slaves and their application to employee rights and conditions? Or do we apply *principles* that we uncover regarding a Christian's submission to their employer that reflects a whole-hearted attitude of fearing the Lord?

Not precisely. The differences are greater than the similarities: masters owned slaves; today's employers don't own employees but hire them; the expectations of obedience and submission is quite different than an employee fulfilling one's job expectations and working hard for an employer; the setting is *Christian* slaves and masters not *secular* settings where Christians often work for non-Christian bosses and Christian bosses also hire non-Christian employees. Furthermore, the reference to receiving an inheritance from the Lord as a reward makes little sense to those who are not slaves, who enjoy rights and privileges, and will often inherit all or part of an estate of a deceased loved one. How do we understand the author's original intended *meaning* and *purpose* and apply their *significance* or the relationship of that meaning to today?[15]

This requires a *theological* reading of Scripture, which focuses on God and his character and standards to shape and improve the beliefs and behaviors of his people in specific ways within a given cultural setting. This is different than trying to discover and then apply principles which underlie the text. A principle is the *level of abstraction* sought to bridge the world of the Bible to the contemporary world by locating the closest point of similarity. So, what preachers or Bible students often do is find a way to apply a fixed text in a more fluid way or ask, "How does this apply to us/me?"

We should ask, "How do we apply the text according to the author's meaning and purpose?" For example, Paul's purpose in Colossians as a whole and in our text on slaves and masters is to establish that believers are to live in Christ Jesus as Lord, surrendered and accountable to him in every area of life in which they are situated. What they believe about Christ (theology) and how they behave in response to those beliefs (practice) corresponds to a change they will exhibit in their cultural setting. For example, this entire section that speaks to wives, husbands, children, slaves, and masters (3:18—4:1) contains a common theological theme—those in superior and those in subservient roles have a mutual responsibility to be subservient to the Lord, and therefore also a *reciprocal obligation* to one another. There is no room for oppression, domination, and lording over those in our households.

This applies particularly to the nuclear family, extended household, and the church family settings, which shape society and the workplace as well, especially where there are issues of the *ownership and control* of others. Obedience and submission, love and justice, are central themes throughout Scripture and in our Colossian text. In addition, the weight of God's favor rests heavily on the side of the poor, the outcast, the oppressed, the alien, the widow, the sick, and the slave. As husbands are over wives, parents are over children, and masters are over slaves, the Lord is over each of them as well. Members of *Christian* households, therefore, must live the gospel transformationally with each other. When each member practices *reciprocal obligation* in the Lord through a magnificent surrender, it will be done in the name of the Lord Jesus

15. Hirsch, *Validity in Interpretation.*

Christ (3:17). When we *put on love* we adorn ourselves with attractive Christian clothing.

REFLECTION FOR GROUPS AND INDIVIDUALS

1. As an individual or group, reflect on and discuss Dallas Willard's quote at the beginning of this chapter. How does Colossians 3:12—4:1 relate?

2. All churches and families have conflict from time to time. Reflect on Colossians 3:12–16. Reflect on the *theological* emphasis of this passage and its practices that will help navigate conflicts in a healthy fashion. List and discuss them. How does gratitude contribute?

PRACTICE FOR GROUPS AND INDIVIDUALS

1. Memorize Colossians 3:12–14. Look for opportunities in your group, church, or family setting to clothe yourself with the virtues listed here, and imagine yourself actually adorned in such clothing, with love as the outer garment. What would you look like? Imagine how you would look if you were clothed with the opposite virtues listed in this passage. Modify your actions this week in light of these virtues.

2. If you are married, read through Colossians 3:18–21 and consult a good commentary. Explore the theological and practical insights that can transform your marriage, family, and parenting. How could this passage assist a young couple that came to you for marriage and parenting counseling? Also consult Ephesians 5:22—6:4.

7

Open Eyes and Open Doors

"Prayer is a subversive act performed in a world that constantly calls faith into question. I may have a sense of estrangement in the very act of prayer, yet by faith I continue to pray and to look for other signs of God's presence."[1]

I SPENT A WEEKEND with a rural evangelical Baptist church of approximately seventy-five people 125 miles northeast of Edmonton. It's a warm and hospitable church situated in a predominantly Catholic community of two hundred in a county of six thousand residents. As in most rural situations, this church has interweaving networks of families and friendships that span decades. In many ways, Pastor Joe there has become the town chaplain. This aging congregation wants to be *missional*, and yet realizes it faces enormous social and spiritual barriers to be a faithful witness for Jesus and the gospel to fellow farmers.

I was scheduled to lead a meeting with the core leaders on Saturday night, and then teach an adult education class and preach on Sunday morning. As I prayed at home before I left, I sensed the Lord didn't want me to arrive with a specific agenda or a prepared talk for the Saturday meeting and the Sunday class. I did plan, however, to preach Romans 12:9–13 for the worship service. During the Saturday night meeting, as we discussed the church and the barriers in the community, it became clear that they had come to a place of frustration, as if a wall blocked their progress. Those were their words. Several mentioned that prayer had been a common subject in the church and many had recently watched a video series on prayer by Jim Cymbala. They realized the only

1. Yancey, *Prayer*, 51.

way forward was through persistent prayer. In the previous year, Joe had also been reading *The Works of Jonathan Edwards* because he longed for revival.

During the Saturday night meeting, I felt prompted to read Colossians 4:2–6. As I commented on the passage, I encouraged these leaders to make "breakthrough prayer" a *central* rather than a bookends practice and priority in their board meetings, annual meetings, worship services, small groups, and virtually every time people gather for study, fellowship, or whatever. I also mentioned that in most churches prayer defaults to an *internal* focus. A common tendency is to pray exclusively for the needs within the church and for each other. We sensed this was a "God moment." We sat in sacred stillness as the Spirit's presence seized our imaginations. This unleashed some lively conversation. We then moved into a vigorous prayer time that lasted about an hour. We met each other, met Scripture, and then God met us!

I then knew what to share with the adult education class for Sunday morning. In the class, I talked about this meeting, commented on Colossians 4:2–6, and then we also prayed! As I preached through Romans 12:9–13 in the worship service, verse 12 seized our attention in an extraordinary way, "Be joyful in hope, patient in affliction, *faithful in prayer.*" I then pronounced, as I've never done before: "If I was a prophet, and I'm not, I would say to you this morning . . . God is calling you to be a church devoted to prayer!" Over the next two weeks the church buzzed about prayer! Breakthrough prayer is part of spiritual warfare. We must move from peaceful malfunction to vigilant mission in prayer. John Piper comments,

> Probably the number one reason why prayer malfunctions in the hands of believers is that we try to turn a wartime walkie-talkie into a domestic intercom. Until you know that life is war, you cannot know what prayer is for. Prayer is for the accomplishment of a wartime mission. . . . We have stopped believing we are in war. No urgency, no watching, no vigilance. No strategic planning. Just easy peace and prosperity.[2]

---

2. Piper, *Let the Nations Be Glad*, 69–70.

PRAYER AND PROCLAMATION

Paul begins to conclude his letter with final instructions to the Colossians in how a magnificent surrender to Jesus as Lord—living in him—must work out in daily life and mission. In chapter 3, he taught how the *inward* practices of heavenly-minded Christians are to live a life of love with one another. He now turns to how the *outward* practices of prayer-devoted Christians are to live a life of witness with non-Christians. This is a *missional spirituality*. His final appeal is for devotion to prayer that also opens the way for clear proclamation, "Devote yourselves to prayer, being watchful and thankful. And pray for us, too, that God may open a door for our message, so that we may proclaim the mystery of Christ, for which I am in chains. Pray that I may proclaim it clearly, as I should" (Col 4:2–4).

We say we believe in prayer, that God answers prayer, and that we need to pray more. We attend prayer meetings, read books on prayer, and "say our prayers." We open and close our meetings with prayer, we ask for "prayer requests," and we say to people: "I'll pray for you." We pray *to* God at prayer meetings, church services, meal times, during "personal devotions," and in times of trial and trauma. Nevertheless, Richard Foster declares, "All who have walked with God have viewed prayer as the main business of their lives."[3] When I look at my life and the life of most churches, I wonder if we truly believe that prayer is the main business of our lives. What I see is endless technocratic brain-numbing study, information, talking, planning, meetings, analysis, and strategies. We tend to rely on man-made methods and models to build and "grow" a church. We learn evangelism techniques and invite people to attend church services and events. These are not all wrong. But perhaps, like the Colossians, we perpetuate a *theological* problem—we don't deeply believe that *Jesus is Lord*—supreme and sufficient. We assume that better leadership and programs will break through the barriers of culture to reach people for Christ.

Paul's appeal to devote ourselves to prayer is the same as that described of the early church, "They *devoted* themselves to the apostles' teaching and to the fellowship, to the breaking of bread and to *prayer*" (Acts 2:42). To be *devoted* means: "Be earnest toward, persist, be constantly diligent, adhere closely." To whom or to what are you devoted?

---

3. Foster, *Celebration of Discipline*, 34.

I'm not sure I can honestly say that I have constant diligence in prayer. I do work at it as a daily discipline more than as a duty. However, a challenge for me is to trust Jesus Christ and not my own competence where he says, "Apart from me you can do nothing" (John 15:5). As an experienced and educated Christian leader, I can recline on the assumption that I'll "get it done." That is, until I slam into stubborn walls of resistance or closed doors of access into people's lives. John Wesley preached, "God will do nothing but in answer to prayer." All significant progress of the Christian movement in the Book of Acts and in church history emerged from earnest devotion to prayer.

Like oxygen, prayer is our primary lifeline to God. Nevertheless, our lives become filled with clutter and clatter. We are busy and preoccupied. Things are noisy. We are tired. We have strenuous jobs. Our children challenge us to the max. We struggle to make ends meet. We wrestle with loneliness and insecurity. We know we should pray, but we find it hard to pray. We stay up late and then sleep in. We feel overwhelmed with all the unfinished jobs around the house and then a parent or a family friend dies. We long for tranquility. Like vertigo, we swirl in a center overrun with intrusive disappointments and losses. We plan to pray someday, when we finally "get it together." But, Dom John Chapman suggests, "Pray as you can, and don't try to pray as you can't" and "the less you pray, the worse it gets."[4] In fact J. C. Ryle remarks, "I ask whether you pray, because neglect of prayer is one great cause of backsliding."[5]

Prayer must also be *watchful* and *thankful*. Like those on guard duty who are alert, we must pray with open eyes. Simone Weil views prayer as "paying absolute unmixed attention" to God. When we are wakeful and thankful in prayer, we practice the discipline of awareness and attention to God and to the times in which we live (Eph 6:18; 1 Thess 5:4–11). This is *outward* prayer as we'll see in verses 3–4. Watchful and thankful prayer fortifies our spirituality. Samuel Zwemer remarks, "Prayer is the gymnasium of the soul." When we are thankful, we are mindful of God's grace as we pay attention to his goodness and generosity in the daily routines of life around us. It's an attitude of gratitude, a mental discipline of awareness that gives credit to God.

4. Chapman, *Spiritual Letters*, 25.

5. J. C. Ryle, "A Call to Prayer," online, http://www.anglicanlibrary.org/ryle/sermon sandtracts/calltoprayer.htm.

Men and women, boys and girls, youth and young adults, must devote themselves to prayer as a spiritual practice of surrender that unleashes God's work. I've seen that largely the North American church and driven people are not devoted to prayer. They are busy, self-reliant, and tired. Prayer can seem boring and ineffective. We discuss problems, decisions, and prayer requests more than we pray about them. We talk too much and pray too little. But Jesus declared, "It is written, 'My house will be called a house of prayer'" (Matt 21:13). And Paul concludes, "Be joyful always; *pray continually*; *give thanks in all circumstances*, for this is God's will for you in Christ Jesus" (1 Thess 5:16–18). We must P.U.S.H.—pray until something happens!

My wife and I are privileged to enjoy a long friendship with Frank and Kathy. They are generous, hospitable, and caring people absolutely devoted to prayer. When we visit them, Frank often prays for us. When we moved from Kelowna to Calgary, Kathy gave us a powerful gift. As she knew that Alberta winters are cold and snowy, she made us a colorful polar fleece blanket. She tied 255-knotted tassels that border the entire blanket. Kathy told us that each tassel stands for a prayer that she offered to God for us as she made the blanket! Many times I've nestled inside that tasseled prayer blanket when I needed Kathy's warmth and God's encouragement. May you regularly blanket others with watchful and thankful prayer attentive to God at work.

Open eyes in prayer will "pay absolute unmixed attention" to open doors for proclamation. Paul's prayer request is a good strategy for our *external* prayers, "And pray for us, too, that God may open a door for our message, so that we may proclaim the mystery of Christ, for which I am in chains. Pray that I may proclaim it clearly, as I should" (vv. 3–4). You can chain Paul to a Roman guard but you can't chain the gospel message. Paul and his apostolic team were on an unstoppable mission. They invited the Colossians to partner with them on that mission too—in prayer, in wise actions, and in gracefully seasoned conversation with *outsiders*. This is missional spirituality in action, which involves risk and outward movement.

On *Facebook*, one of my friends posted the following: "The challenge for many church leaders comes down to working with people who like comfort, predictability and sameness more than risk, faith, and forward movement. It is odd to me that God dealt with this throughout history. What causes God's people to treasure comfort over His calling and commission?" One person offered the following response: "I think it has to do with the model of church I've seen cultivated in my lifetime. When the model is based on attraction and getting a person to a place, then it makes it harder to get them to see faith as a journey. When we use the church as a destination, then it tends to become a final stop." We must see ourselves as sent ones, who pray for open doors for the gospel as we also embody it with our character and our conversation.

As we share our faith, like Paul, we'll encounter many closed hearts and minds of defiant people who oppose God's word. Only God can open a door for our message (1 Cor 16:9; 2 Cor 2:12). We can deliver this word through all verbal forms of communication (v. 3) as we reveal the mystery of Christ clearly as we should (v. 4). However, we shouldn't try to manufacture opportunities and we can't force people to listen or welcome what we have to say. This gospel message comes to people, as a dynamic force, able to bear fruit and grow (Col 1:6).

Some call this prayer evangelism, based on intercession and godly action. We can pray into our neighborhoods and communities, schools and workplaces, and through our networks of family and friends. With breakthrough prayer, we can regularly ask God to open doors of opportunity for us to share Christ and the hope that lies within us. Residents can pray for their communities; mother's can pray for their kid's schoolteachers; businessmen can pray for their employees or customers. We can all pray for non-Christian family members and neighbors. A few years ago, I began to pray Colossians 4:2–6 regularly. A couple of months later, my wife's brother and wife invited us over for dinner. During the after dinner discussion, the topic of "religion" came up and we saw an open door of opportunity to clearly communicate our faith to them. They invited it! Recently, we've also had conversations with our next-door neighbors.

I've had the opportunity to teach several Tuesday evening courses at Alberta Bible College in their PACE (Professional Adult Career Education) degree program. I get to meet many outstanding students who come from all walks of life. One of those students was Shannon. She and her husband Frank drive a rig together every week hauling materials from Calgary to Texas. They return in time for her Tuesday classes. Below is a story she shares about one of her road trips and how Colossians 4:2–6 relates. She calls it "On the Road to Divine Opportunities."

In the past ten years of being a team professional driver with my husband, the Lord has provided many divine encounters. Colossians 4:2–6 has been vital because we have learned to be prepared to share our faith and the love of Jesus in unlikely settings.

A very memorable encounter that happened recently involved a United States Customs and Border Protection officer. Because we are on a dedicated run each week, we generally cross at the same border. However, last fall, our weekly routing was changed, and it was very unusual, because our logistics coordinators requested that we head west for an extra load and then pick up our southbound freight out of a terminal that was not commonly accessed by team drivers. This added extra miles and extra time to our schedule, making it a bit of a challenge to make our Texas delivery. But, we have learned that when something out of the ordinary occurs, it's because the Lord has a distinct plan.

On this trip we were to cross at a smaller U.S. port, one that we have utilized maybe six times in our ten years of driving. After preparing the paperwork for this crossing, it's mandatory for the drivers to go in to the border building to see customs and immigration agents. I had been praying before arriving at this particular port because I sensed that God had something in store for us, and asked him to give us the words to speak. Because I knew that we would have to stay with the agents until a search and inspection of both the tractor and trailer were completed, I asked the Lord to grant us favor and to use us as he saw fit.

When we handed our identification to Officer J. he commented that my hair had grown since my last card photo. Before I could think of a response, I heard my husband say that I had cut it off when my mother was diagnosed with cancer and I had gone to take care of her. The agent quietly asked me if she had survived, and I told him that she had not. This was a personal conversation and very awkward because of the environment we were in. I could see that an immigration officer and another customs agent were watching us. Officer J. proceeded to tell us that his thirteen-year old son was just diagnosed with cancer that afternoon (we arrived at the border three hours after he had received the news), and he was waiting for another phone call from his wife after speaking to a specialist. He told us he did not know what they were going to do. He tried to maintain a "professional" demeanor, but he seemed compelled to speak with us about his family.

Immediately, I found myself telling him my story of how God had healed me of malignant melanoma, and I shared the faith stance my husband and I had taken. He asked me if we had gone to the Mayo Clinic, and my husband told Officer J. that we had prayed and believed God would heal me and that I did not undergo any form of chemo or radiation therapy because of the type of cancer I had. I told the agent that we would pray for him and his family, and I asked for his son's first name. This was very difficult for me because we were in a high security setting, and protocol dictates that one waits quietly for the officers to do their job, never asking for personal information from an agent.

I sensed that God had brought us to Officer J. to share the hope of Christ and the love God has for people. Without hesitation, Officer J. told us his son's name, thanked us for praying, and expressed his gratitude that we were so open with him. He also stated that he would be contacting his community church to have them pray for his son, as he was encouraged because of my healing. We were with this officer for about thirty minutes. This "hurting dad" shared his pain with a couple of anonymous truck drivers, and we shared the hope we had in Jesus as Lord. For us, this encounter confirmed that we are God's servants called to keep our eyes open for open doors of opportunity, to proclaim the message clearly, and to act wisely toward those outside the faith. We are determined to serve God as truck drivers devoted to prayer and thanksgiving![6]

CONDUCT AND CONVERSATION

In our book *Missional Spirituality*, my co-author Len and I conclude with a chapter entitled, "The Gospel According to You." The basic point is this: our walk must match our talk; our behavior must match our beliefs. We are living letters as local missionaries. We all fail; we're all imperfect; but unbelievers are acutely sensitive to hypocrisy. Gandhi remarked, "I like your Christ; I do not like your Christians. Your Christians are so unlike your Christ." Unbelievers will only read the gospel according to Roger when I have Christlike conduct and conversation. Paul ends with a crucial warning, "Be wise in the way you act toward outsiders; make the most of every opportunity. Let your conversation be always full of

---

6. Used by permission.

grace, seasoned with salt, so that you may know how to answer everyone" (Col 4:5–6).

There's an interconnected relationship between our prayers, our proclamation, and our actions—they must all match. If we are obstinate, we can burn a Koran to incite a theological protest. But we can also burn a bridge to Muslims by this irrevocable foolishness. People observe our lives. We are to literally "walk in wisdom," or live wisely, as we display a full life with the knowledge of God's will through all spiritual wisdom and understanding (Col 1:9). This can only occur to the extent that we practice a magnificent surrender to Jesus as Lord. The power of his presence must permeate our conduct and conversation. Watchful prayer and wise actions labor as subversive partners. Like yeast, they work in subtle and transforming ways. It's tempting to take matters into our own hands and orchestrate ways to share our faith or defend Christianity's truth claims. Jim Wallis states, "The only way to propagate a message is to live it."[7]

We should always be on the lookout to make the most of every opportunity that might present itself as an open door for our message. People are interested in God and spirituality, though not so much in the institutional church. God is at work in the world. But we can become an obstacle to our own message if we aren't wise in how we act. There are times where I offended unbelievers that I worked with and more than once offended my father-in-law and mother-in-law! It's difficult to maintain a consistent spiritual example when we're tired, frustrated, angry, or busy. People can't hear our words if our actions yell otherwise. When we act wisely and speak winsomely with gracious and seasoned words that flow from a gracious heart (Matt 12:34), we'll gain a better hearing. Unbelievers raise innocent and sometimes hostile questions about God, Jesus, the Bible, and Christianity. Our responsibility is to be messengers who adorn the message with charming actions and winsome speech. This puts us in a better place to know how to answer everyone. Peter likewise encouraged, "Always be prepared to give an answer to everyone who asks you to give the reason for the hope that you have. But do this with gentleness and respect" (1 Pet 3:15). Be prepared and prayerful, and act wisely with outsiders.

N. T. Wright offers a concluding remark before we move to the last part of Colossians 4, "Paul's thought has come full circle. Beginning with a report of his thankful prayer for the Colossians (1:3ff.), and of

7. Wallis, *Call to Conversion*, 116.

his work for the gospel (1:24—2:5), he has ended with the request that they should pray as he prays, and work as he works. Their prayer and life, like his, are to be expressions of the loving wisdom of God, reaching out in Christ to save the world."[8] In effect, this is missional spirituality in action, where our spiritual life in Christ feeds and forms our missional life for Christ. Below is an email that I recently received from a woman who listened to a sermon I preached in a church service in Calgary on Colossians 4:2–6:

> Roger, thanks for your encouraging sermon. I have certainly been learning the truth of the need to devote myself to prayer! I have been dealing with osteoarthritis, resulting in muscle spasms and pain for the past two to three years. I usually wake up two to six times each night because of pain, so I have been thanking God for "quality quiet time with him" and asking him to bring people to mind who need prayer and blessing. It's amazing how many people and situations I can pray for through the night! I do what I can through exercise, physiotherapy and prayer for my back, but otherwise, I choose to thank God. I had several family phone calls this weekend. I have a brother whose marriage is split right now; a sister who is going through a major depression; a brother-in-law who is finishing work on the family house, to sell it and move where his wife and three girls are living; and a mother-in-law who is bitter about it all.
>
> I want you to know how right on the mark this Colossians text was for me personally. I'm constantly praying, "Lord, let my conversation be always full of grace, seasoned with salt, so that I may know how to answer everyone" (Col 4:6). I had a five-hour conversation with my sister Friday night and she wants to hear God her way. I was able to be gentle and I think "grace filled" but the salt comes from my own life and sharing how I see my pain, work and prayer life right now. She is experiencing depression and a host of other physical problems. She has had a Christian faith in the past, but seems to want to piece together all the aspects that "work for her" and reject the hard bits that don't fit in with her life-philosophy. I am praying not just "how to answer everyone" but that God would soften their hearts and open doors for them to hear!

Benedict of Nursia, Italy (ca. 480–547) was a layman who founded the Benedictine Order and his *Rule* (a way of life), with its seventy-three

---

8. N. T. Wright, *Colossians and Philemon*, 154.

chapters available online.[9] Though fifteen hundred years old, *The Rule of Benedict* continues to be a spiritual guide in the Western world that appeals to average people.[10] Benedictine spirituality does not emphasize the devotional life of the individual as much as that formed in community. Its highly social dimension shows how to live with others and how to treat guests. The *Rule* is holistic as it celebrates ordinary life as comprised of one piece with "prayer and work"—*ora et labora*—as a motto. It nurtures a spiritual life to be lived in the real world with a missionary spirit. Benedict prescribed a four-fold system for the sacred reading of Scripture called *lectio divina*, which enjoys a resurgence of interest today in missional and spiritual formation literature. Benedict celebrated silence and obedience as virtues, and placed the twelve steps of *humility* at the center of his *Rule*. The art of *listening* to Scripture, to the Rule, to one another, and to the world around us is the core spiritual practice. Make Benedict's prayer your own:

> O gracious and holy Father,
> Give us wisdom to perceive You,
> Intelligence to understand You,
> Diligence to seek You,
> Patience to wait for You,
> Eyes to behold You,
> A heart to meditate upon You,
> And a life to proclaim You;
> Through the power of the Spirit of
> Jesus Christ our Lord.

REFLECTION FOR GROUPS AND INDIVIDUALS

1. What does it mean to *devote* yourself to prayer being watchful and thankful? Describe your experiences in prayer, both positive and negative. Bring other passages of Scripture into the discussion that speak to the practice of continual, persevering, watchful, and thankful prayer and how to cultivate it as a group and as an individual.

---

9. *The Rule of Benedict*, online: http://www.osb.org/rb/text/toc.html.

10. See Wil Derkse, *The Rule of Benedict for Beginners*, and Joan Chittister, *Wisdom Distilled From the Daily: Living the Rule of St. Benedict Today.*

2. Discuss how you see the need for "breakthrough prayer," where God must open a door for our message in your situations at your workplace, in your family, and in your community. Also, discuss the many different ways you can share the message of the mystery of Christ (the gospel) and how to proclaim it clearly as you should.

PRACTICE FOR GROUPS AND INDIVIDUALS

1. Memorize Colossians 4:2–6. Pray it through regularly. Thank God for specific things in your life for which you are grateful. Pray specifically for and be alert to ways in which God is at work and for doors of opportunity that also open for you to share the message of the gospel.

2. Monitor how you act when in the presence of unbelievers. Imagine yourself as a wise and thoughtful person, embedded in the world as salt and light, whose conduct and conversation are subversive influences for God's presence wherever you are. Monitor your conversation and your words, and how ready you are to give an answer to those who ask about your faith.

8

Friends and Fellows

*"Communitas, not community, is the adventure and
comradeship experienced in all phenomenal Jesus movements.
It describes a social togetherness and belonging that occurs with
a group of people, who inspired by the vision of a better world,
gather around a common mission."*[1]

THE GREEK CITY-STATE, *POLIS*, had an interesting way to call its
citizens together when it needed a vote for some type of action. If,
for example, another city-state marched against them for battle, a person would walk the streets blowing a horn to announce that all should
gather in the amphitheater just outside of town. When the citizens of the
city heard this, they would close their shops, head to the amphitheater to
hear the news, and fulfill their civic duty with their response. However,
some shop-owners refused to close down as they hoped to take advantage of extra business while the competitor's businesses were closed. The
Greeks referred to such persons as *idiotes* (idiots). This term referred to
those who, closed up in their own world concerned only for themselves,
ignored the greater political and public good of the community.[2]

Paul's concluding greetings, which mention eleven people in
Colossians 4:7–18, contain no *idiotes* (except Demas). Rather, they contain a compelling glimpse into the social dynamics of Christian *communitas*—the camaraderie and common family life formed around Christ's
mission. In staccato like fashion, Paul offers a stately commentary on
prized people whom he regarded as friends and fellow servants. They

1. Hirsch, *The Forgotten Ways*, 217–22.
2. Wilkins and Sanford, *Hidden Worldviews*, 30.

were faithful—full of faith—members of the Jesus movement marked by sacrificial service for God's kingdom, magnificently surrendered to Christ and his mission. Terms of endearment and commendation abound. Of course, they're all dead and gone now but their names and reputations live on. In late 2011, we learned that renowned *New York Times* respected theologian John Stott died at age ninety. His name lives on. How's your name?

FRIENDS AND FELLOW SERVANTS

Have you ever mused on what people think of you? When my name pops up, I wonder what words fitly describe how others experience me—especially my family and colleagues? In my book *The Journey,* I open chapter 1 with the following reflection that still challenges me:

> Have you attended many funerals? I have. Reflect for a moment on what they are like. Our reflection will depend on the relationship we had with the people we came to respect. During a funeral with its program compressed into minutes, we attempt to honor a life composed of years. We grieve the loss. Our hearts scramble to deal with how brutal and final death feels. As we sing familiar hymns and listen to the sermon, we struggle to absorb brief moments of comfort. But more than all of this, for me, a convicting interrogation occurs deep inside my heart. As I choke back the tears while I hear kind words spoken about the person, I hear other words spoken to *me,* "What about *you* Roger? What will they say at *your* funeral? How are you living *your* life?" I become very sober about *my* death. Even more sober about *my* life. I'm reminded, *it's not how you start the journey that counts; it's how you finish.*[3]

Someone said, "Good people must die, but death cannot kill their names." To have your name permanently etched into the Bible would be a supreme honor for those whose lives are commended rather than critiqued. As Annie Dillard mused, "How we spend our days is, of course, how we spend our lives."[4] The church consists of real people. The apostolic mission of Paul and Timothy to the Colossians involved many common companions of the faith. Writing while imprisoned, Paul singles out people he knew who had good names—honorable and

---

3. Helland, *The Journey,* 23 (italics in the original).

4. Dillard, *The Writing Life,* 32.

faithful people. His affectionate language shows that he and the early church enjoyed spiritual relationships with terms associated with family, friendship, and fellow servanthood. Paul had no shortage of spiritual comrades and associates. The spiritual glue that bound them together wasn't church vision, structure, or position. It was deep spiritual relationship in *communitas*.

The first person Paul named is his missional courier Tychicus (4:7). Also mentioned in Acts 20:4, 2 Timothy 4:12, and Titus 3:12, Paul calls him a "dear brother, a faithful minister and fellow servant in the Lord" (Col 4:7). Tychicus was a known and trusted family member in the household of faith—literally "the beloved brother." He was not a minister according to today's term used for clergy, but a faithful servant and fellow slave of Jesus Christ. Paul sent this trusted man without title or position to the Colossians, so he would inform them about Paul's circumstances in prison and also encourage their hearts (4:8). Onesimus, a fellow Colossian turned Christian and Philemon's one time runaway slave, would also accompany Tychicus. Paul also calls Onesimus a faithful and dear brother (4:9–10). A magnificent surrender will transform us into dear people who are faithful servants and slaves of the Lord Jesus Christ.

Next, Paul conveys special greetings from six of his coworkers. Three were Jews and three were Gentiles. The Jews were: Aristarchus, Mark, and Jesus called Justus (4:10–11). Aristarchus, a fellow prisoner who "did time" together with Paul, sent his greetings, as did Mark, the cousin of Barnabas (4:10). Aristarchus, a Macedonian from Thessalonica and one of Paul's traveling companions, was with him during the riot at the Temple of Diana in Ephesus (Acts 19:29; 20:4). He also accompanied Paul when he sailed to Rome as a prisoner (Acts 27:2). Aristarchus proved to be a loyal traveling companion who also knew the Colossians. Paul was not alone in jail. Through thick and thin Aristarchus stuck closer to him than a brother.

Then there's Mark. You likely remember the story of the falling out between Paul and Barnabas over Mark. On the second missionary journey, Barnabas wanted to take his cousin John (also called Mark) along with Paul to visit the brothers in all the towns where they had preached the word of the Lord and see how they were doing (Acts 15:36–37). But, "Paul did not think it wise to take him, because he had deserted them in Pamphylia and had not continued with them in the work" (Acts 15:38).

This refers to the incident on the first missionary journey when he and Barnabas took Mark with them as their helper. But in the middle of the journey John Mark deserted them and returned to Jerusalem (Acts 13:5, 13). It seems Paul could not find it in his heart to forgive him for such a deplorable decision. After all, to a team of fellow soldiers in the heat of battle, desertion is the lowest form of betrayal.

When Barnabas wanted to take John Mark along on the second missionary journey, he and Paul had such a sharp disagreement over it that they parted company never to work together again. Barnabas took Mark and sailed for Cyprus while Paul chose Silas and headed for Syria and Cilicia to strengthen the churches (Acts 15:37–41). However, twelve years later, Paul told the Colossians that they received instructions about Mark and to welcome him if he came to them (Col 4:10). We don't know what transpired in the interim. We do know that Mark was with Paul during his imprisonment, and in the letter to Philemon, he called him his *fellow worker* as with Aristarchus (Philemon 24). In his final days Paul wrote to Timothy, "Only Luke is with me. Get Mark and bring him with you, because he is helpful to me in my ministry" (2 Tim 4:11).

Somehow, Paul finally had a change of heart. Perhaps Mark's leadership showed signs of growth and maturity. Perhaps time healed an old wound. We all do and say things that are equivalent to desertion, disloyalty, or delinquency. Paul affirmed Mark to the Colossians and made a way for grace and acceptance to prevail. There's room for disagreements. I've pastored in three different churches where at times I felt like a self-justified Paul or Barnabas, and even a self-compromised Mark. Perhaps you have felt the same. What's our responsibility? If we are like Barnabas, let us encourage with grace. If we are like Paul, let us acknowledge someone's growth. If we are like Mark, let us be a helper in ministry. God's kingdom can sustain such personal failures and foibles. There's room for parting of ways where the work of Christ will relentlessly continue, even on two separate trajectories. But on the horizon the two rails of the train track will eventually meet in Christ and his cause. This is true Christian *communitas*.

The third Jew to send greetings is Jesus, also called Justus (4:11). That's all we know of him. Jesus was a common name among first century Jews before Jesus Christ was widely known in the second century. Common, ordinary, yet faithful people comprise God's kingdom—the Janes and Johns of everyday life. Paul concludes, "These are the only

Jews among my fellow workers for the kingdom of God, and they have proved a comfort to me" (4:11). Pastors and parishioners tend to view the work of ministry as work *inside the institutional church*. Seminaries tend to train today's clergy for *church work*—theology, hermeneutics, leadership and administration, preaching, and counseling. These are not wrong, just limited.

Jesus and the early church concerned themselves with *kingdom* work *outside*. God is on mission—the *missio Dei*. God the Father sent his Son on mission to seek and save lost people and invite them to surrender to his rule as Lord and follow him. Matthew concludes, "Jesus went throughout Galilee, teaching in their synagogues, preaching the good news of the kingdom, and healing every disease and sickness among the people" and large crowds followed him (Matt 4:23–25). Jesus sent his church on mission to continue his kingdom work. Luke concludes, "For two whole years Paul stayed there [in Rome] in his own rented house and welcomed all who came to see him. Boldly and without hindrance he preached the kingdom of God and taught about the Lord Jesus Christ" (Acts 28:30–31).

Jesus did not call people to enter the *church* but to enter the *kingdom*. Of course, the church is God's primary instrument to serve as a sign, foretaste, and messenger of his kingdom. Jesus is Lord of his church. Christ followers are called to surrender to his authority and purposes. But the work of the kingdom does not mean church work per sé. I can volunteer for youth, children's, small groups, and teaching ministries. I can serve on boards or committees; lead Bible studies and Alpha or Vacation Bible Schools. I can go on summer mission trips or become a pastor or denominational leader. I can even commit to spiritual formation and holiness. However, I can do all these and not do kingdom work at all. What's the work of kingdom ministry? It's to proclaim and practice the rule and reign of God over all dimensions of our life and invite and influence others to do likewise. The heart of kingdom work is a magnificent surrender to Christ Jesus who is both *Lord and Messiah*. Acts 2:36 announces to Israel and the world, "Let all Israel be assured of this: God has made this Jesus, whom you crucified, both Lord and Messiah."

Paul moves from the three Jews whom he regarded as fellow workers of God's kingdom and a comfort to him, to three Gentiles starting with Epaphras, who sent greetings as "one of you" (4:12). He first appears in Colossians 1:7 where Paul identifies him as a Colossian resident and local missionary through whom the Colossians learned the gospel. His character is exemplary. His name lives on as someone known as a dear fellow servant, faithful minister, and servant of Christ Jesus who is always wrestling (agonizing) in prayer for them (4:12). It's hard to fathom the spiritual depth of people like Epaphras. Earnest, struggling, agonizing prayer dwells and flourishes at the core of hard kingdom work. It's laser focused on God through local servants like Epaphras and other Christians like him.

If you want to hunker down and contend in prayer like an Olympic athlete in training, pray like Epaphras, "That you [and your church] may stand firm in all the will of God, mature [*teleios*] and fully assured." Remember our word *telos*? It's something complete and mature, having reached its end goal. When we stand firm, entirely cemented in God's will, we become mature and enter a settled state of complete confidence while in it. For all the fascination and fixation on church health and growth, nothing will produce a mature church like standing firm in the whole will of God, period. And we should wrestle in prayer to that end.

Swiss Reformed theologian Karl Barth remarks, "The first and basic act of theological work is *prayer*. . . . Theological work is also *study*; in every respect it is also *service*; and finally it would certainly be in vain were it not also an act of love."[5] Christian leadership is largely learning how to lead in the work of Christian theology, in prayer and in practice. I must not work at theology merely as academics but as spiritual formation and service, sustained by prayer and motivated by love. In a similar way, Eugene Peterson writes that there are three angles that pastors must work at: 1) prayer, 2) Scripture, and 3) spiritual direction.[6] Epaphras worked painfully hard not only for the Colossians but also for those in nearby Laodicea (twelve miles west) and Hierapolis (fifteen miles northwest) (4:13). His kingdom work seemed to include not only earnest prayer but also some sort of district pastoral service for this triangle of cities.

The last two Gentiles to send their greetings through Paul to the Colossians were Luke the doctor and Demas the defector (4:14). Paul's "dear friend Luke," mentioned by name and profession here, is also mentioned in Philemon 24, and in 2 Timothy 4:11 where Paul remarks, "Only Luke is with me." Tradition holds that he's the author—and the

---

5. Barth, *Evangelical Theology*, 160 (italics in the original).

6. Peterson, *Working the Angles*.

only Gentile author in the New Testament—of the great two-volume work known as the Gospel of Luke and the Acts of the Apostles. They together comprise nearly one fourth of the New Testament. His true significance as a missional companion of Paul hides in the background of the "we" passages in the book of Acts, where an author includes himself in the story. Luke would have experienced much of what he wrote about there. Douglas Moo comments,

> We can conclude that he was a regular companion of Paul, participating with him in ministry in Macedonia (Acts 16:8–17), on his trip back to Palestine after the third missionary journey (Acts 20:5–15; 21:1–18), and on the 'shipwreck' voyage to Rome (Acts 27:1—28:16). So it would be natural to think that Luke stayed on with Paul in Rome during his imprisonment there.[7]

Unfortunately, the same can't be said of Demas, whom Paul once considered a *fellow worker* (Phlm 24). When Paul wrote to Timothy just a few years later, we learn of an all too common failure in faith, "Do your best to come to me quickly, for Demas, because he loved this world, has deserted me and has gone to Thessalonica. Crescens has gone to Galatia, and Titus to Dalmatia. Only Luke is with me. Get Mark and bring him with you, because he is helpful to me in my ministry. I sent Tychicus to Ephesus" (2 Tim 4:9–12). Even though Paul enjoyed the company of faithful friends, some people disagreed with or deserted him, or departed to other ministry assignments. Fellowship is sometimes fractured. We all suffer from severed relationships. Because Demas "loved this world" he deserted Paul. That's a stinging indictment. We could say that though he did not start out this way, Demas finished as an *idiotes*.

Are you, or am I, in any way enticed or ensnared by the sensual, oppressive, consumer-oriented, arrogant, and Satan-infected world devoid of God's love? When we don't know what to do if we slide into such squalor, here are our instructions to avoid becoming an idiotes:

> Do not love the world or anything in the world. If anyone loves the world, the love of the Father is not in him. For everything in the world—the cravings of sinful man, the lust of his eyes and the boasting of what he has and does—comes not from the Father but from the world. The world and its desires pass away, but the man who does the will of God lives forever. (1 John 2:15–17)

7. Moo, *The Letters to the Colossians and to Philemon*, 347.

I know a few fellow workers who not only deserted me, but also deserted the Lord Jesus Christ. They surrendered, rather, to the world. The lure of the world coupled with the deeply ingrained personal problems that people contend with, are enough to sidetrack the strongest Christians. In his allegory *The Pilgrim's Progress*, incarcerated English preacher John Bunyan depicts the trials and temptations that assault Christians on their way to the Celestial City. They must go through the town of Vanity that holds a year-round fair called Vanity Fair.

It's a place contrived by Beelzebub (chief lord of the fair), Apollyon, and Legion. This fair provides every kind of entertainment and sells merchandise, popularity, position, titles, games, votes, artificial personalities, sex appeal, and prostitutes. It offers gambling, cheating, drinking, stealing, adulteries, and all kinds of immoralities. In the town are also taverns, night-clubs, roadhouses, seductive shows, casinos, fashionable churches, and racketeers. Evangelist says to them (and us), "But if anyone going to the Celestial City would miss this town of Vanity, he must of necessity go out of the world" (see 1 Cor 4:10). When Christian and Faithful entered the fair and were asked to buy the goods, "they would stop their ears and say, 'Turn away my eyes from beholding vanity,' looking upward as if they belonged to another country."[8]

FINAL GREETINGS AND INSTRUCTIONS

We now approach the conclusion of Paul's deeply theological yet practical letter to the Colossians, designed to encourage its hearers and readers to live in the Lord. He waits until the end to send his own personal greetings and final instructions (4:15–18). It's a detailed glimpse into the personal correspondence of this great apostle. Though Paul writes his greeting in his own hand while imprisoned in chains (4:18), his mind is ever active with pointed instructions for groups and individuals. Though his body was confined to Roman imprisonment, his heart was concerned about his Christian family. He affectionately addressed them as "the holy and faithful brothers in Christ at Colosse" (1:2) and concluded with, "Give my greetings to the brothers at Laodicea, and to Nympha and the church in her house. After this letter has been read to you, see that it is also read in the church of the Laodiceans and that you in turn read the letter from

---

8. Bunyan, *The Pilgrim's Progress: in Today's English*, 89–90.

Laodicea" (4:15–16). We don't know the identity of this letter, but it was to be read in Colossae.

Known for its wealth and for its medical school that formulated a spice nard for the treatment of ears and an eye salve, Laodicea became a more prominent city than Colossae. However, it lacked a decent water supply like the hot springs of Hierapolis and the cold waters of Colossae. Although Paul had not personally visited the church there, it was still as important to him as the Colossians, as he wanted the churches in both places to exchange letters. Laodicea eventually came under the scope of Christ's correction when he warned them:

> I know your deeds, that you are neither cold nor hot. I wish you were either one or the other! So, because you are lukewarm—neither hot nor cold—I am about to spit you out of my mouth. You say, 'I am rich; I have acquired wealth and do not need a thing.' But you do not realize that you are wretched, pitiful, poor, blind and naked. I counsel you to buy from me gold refined in the fire, so you can become rich; and white clothes to wear, so you can cover your shameful nakedness; and salve to put on your eyes, so you can see. (Rev 3:15–18)

It must have been difficult for the early church to remember and apply the pertinent truths in Scripture that were read to them publicly. People did not own personal printed copies of Paul's letters, or the collection of letters, which centuries later would become the complete canon of the New Testament. God's word is living and active not confined to print. It must live in the hearts and minds of his people by the Spirit. Neither the church at Laodicea nor at Colossae exists today. Nevertheless, all churches that exist today are subject to the same cultural and worldly values as the Colossians and Laodiceans and need Paul's letter just as much.

Also noteworthy, is that Paul knew of and extended his personal greetings to a woman named Nympha and the church that met in her house. Until the third century, the church did not own property nor did it construct its own buildings in which to meet. It was more natural and practical to meet in the homes of its members and leaders. Many churches have started in homes, and of course, there's the house church movement, and more recently a movement to establish *missional communities*. The Christian faith seems to thrive best in relational webs of family, friends, neighborhoods, networks, and small groups, in *communitas*. Thank God for women (and men and couples) who offer their hospitality and their homes to support the Lord's mission. Many Christian women are the backbone of many churches with prayer, care, and hospitality.

Finally, Paul instructs, "Tell Archippus: 'See to it that you complete the work you have received in the Lord'" (4:17). Apparently, Paul got wind of a special ministry task (*diakonian*) that Archippus needed to accomplish for the church at Colossae. We don't know what it was, but as a good mentor would do, Paul felt it was important enough to exhort Archippus. We know that Archippus was a Colossian and member of Philemon's household, and considered a *fellow soldier* by Paul (Phlm 2). As a fellow soldier, engaged in the battles of spiritual warfare and in service for the Lord, Archippus needed to fulfill these *in the Lord*. All kingdom service regarded as Christian must be completed in union with the Lord, in magnificent surrender to him.

In the summer of 2011, I attended a convention of a denomination whose future and whose seminary is uncertain in terms of their viability and sustainability. I have also been working with a large church that is conflicted with chronic spiritual, leadership, and structural issues. Most denominations and churches in the West these days face a crisis of trying to figure out how to unfreeze themselves from institutional dullness and recover a sense of mission, leadership, holiness, and renew themselves spiritually and structurally. But many denominations and churches face a greater *theological* crisis of what it means to be the people of God, in magnificent surrender to Jesus Christ as Lord, who radically *live* in him through faith and not just intellectually believe in him through doctrine. The colossal *Christology* displayed in Colossians can inform us and inspire us to practice faith as an active trust in the person of Christ and his mission in the world. As we've worked through this last section of Colossians, do you sense the depth of spiritual friendship, the quality of spiritual character, and the camaraderie of spiritual *communitas*? Does this list of faithful friends and fellows, who serve, pray, and work hard in the Lord challenge and inspire you? It inspires and challenges me.

With all the buzz about the *missional church* these days, we must not view this in abstract ways as just another church style like seeker church, teaching church, evangelistic church, caring church, breakout church, or simple church. A missional church is only that when missional *people* comprise it—as a group of disciples who actually believe who Jesus is, obey what Jesus taught, and live in Jesus as Lord as sent ones on mission with him in the world. In our book *Missional Spirituality*, Len and I show how Christian spirituality is vitally connected to mission and grounded theologically in the Trinity, the Incarnation, the priesthood of all believers, and in the great commandment to love God and neighbor from the inside out. We must embody and express our theology. We offer tangible *practices* that can help shape us into missional people who love God from all our heart, soul, mind, and strength, and our neighbor as our self.[9] Dear reader, see to it that you complete the work you have received in the Lord, and may God's grace be with you. May you know the riches of living in the Lord and the glorious inheritance of his people. Because of your faith in the Lord Jesus and your love for all the saints, like Paul:

> I keep asking that the God of our Lord Jesus Christ, the glorious Father, may give you the Spirit of wisdom and revelation, so that you may know him better. I pray also that the eyes of your heart may be enlightened in order that you may know the hope to which he has called you, the riches of his glorious inheritance in the saints, and his incomparably great power for us who believe. (Eph 1:17–19)

REFLECTION FOR GROUPS AND INDIVIDUALS

1. Reflect on and discuss the idea of *communitas*. How is it different than simply Christian community? How might Colossians 4:7–18 contribute to your understanding of *communitas* and what it takes for it to occur in your context?

2. Read through and discuss the personal characteristics of Tychicus (4:7), Onesimus (4:9), and Epaphras (4:12–13). Plumb the depths of what is said about each of them and look them up in other places in the New Testament. What characteristics challenge or inspire you and why?

3. Consider Demas and how he once had a good name as a "fellow soldier" of Paul, but eventually deserted him because he loved the world. Reflect on what it means to love the world and evaluate the extent to which the world entices or has possibly ensnared you and what it will take to overcome that.

---

9. See Helland and Hjalmarson, *Missional Spirituality*.

PRACTICE FOR GROUPS AND INDIVIDUALS

1. Select regular times when alone or in a group setting to *wrestle* in prayer for your church, to stand firm in all the will of God, mature and fully assured.

2. Consider how you may start a missional community in your home. Do a Google search on "missional community" and review the websites and *Wikipedia* article. Purchase an available book, primer, or field guide to help you.

3. Practice kingdom theology where you daily submit your life to God's rule, and missional spirituality, where you daily seek to love God and your neighbor, in magnificent surrender to Jesus as Lord.

Conclusion: Jesus Is Life

"All men of the modern world exist in a continual and flagrant antagonism between their consciences and their way of life."[1]

HENRI NOUWEN, IN HIS book *With Open Hands*, tells the story of an elderly woman brought to a psychiatric center. She was wild and would swing at everything in sight frightening everyone. The doctors had to take everything away from her. However, she gripped onto a small coin in her tight fist and wouldn't let go. It took two people to pry open her clenched fist. It was as if she would lose her very self and give up her last bit of security and control along with the coin. As she held onto the coin she also held onto her fear. Nouwen remarks, "When you are invited to pray, you are asked to open your tightly clenched fist and give up your last coin. But who wants to do that? You feel it is safer to cling to a sorry past than to trust in a new future. So, you fill your hands with small, clammy coins which you don't want to surrender."[2]

This sad image depicts a prevalent issue for many of us. We cling to our clammy insecurities and our entrenched fears because our faith in the supreme and sufficient Lord Jesus Christ is frail. Do you recall Matthew 6:25–34, where Jesus teaches us to not worry about even the basic necessities of life? He reminds us that God feeds the birds and clothes the grass and will likewise look after us because we are so much more valuable than they are. But those of us under our heavenly Father's care, who worry, have a more fundamental issue. Jesus labels us as those "of little faith" (v. 30). In a startling revelation, he remarks that *pagans* are the ones who worry about what they will eat and drink and what they will wear (v. 32)! Instead, God's people are to seek first his kingdom and righteousness and to not worry about the future. We must "grow out of

---

1. Tolstoy, *The Kingdom of God is Within You*, 136.
2. Nouwen, *With Open Hands*, 20–21.

control" and practice a magnificent surrender—like prayer with open hands.

Why is it so hard to surrender to Jesus Christ as Lord? If we've interpreted the book of Colossians correctly, isn't it because our actual view of Jesus Christ and our knowledge of God are stunted? And isn't this because we don't actually *practice* our theology? Why would we not open our clenched fist that clutches one measly coin to receive the boundless riches and treasures available in Christ? Why would we allow the hollow yet enticing philosophies of a Christless culture shape us into its image rather than into the image of Christ? Why would we set our hearts and minds on a littered Hollywood street rather than on Jesus Christ who sits at God's right hand in the heavenly palace? Is it because we settle for an intellectual belief in Christ Jesus as our Lord that results in malpractice when it comes to Christ Jesus as our Life? Paul's pungent theological statement should transform our worldview and practice, "When Christ, *who is your life*, appears, then you also will appear with him in glory" (Col 3:4). He does not say, Christ who is your belief system, your creed, or your doctrine. Christ is our *life*. Paul's central point in Colossians is, "So then, just as you received Christ Jesus as Lord, continue to live in him" (Col 2:6). Peter drives the point home, "But in your hearts set apart Christ as Lord" (1 Pet 3:15).

When I began to write this book, I invited my friends on *Facebook* to read through Colossians and offer their personal reflections. A friend who lives near Vancouver that I've known for many years offered hers. She is an amazing woman full of faith and wonder, a professional photographer, a mother of three girls, a loyal friend to my wife and me, and a fellow servant of Jesus Christ. Her name is Lorna. The crucial thing about her is that she recently spent the better part of an entire year battling leukemia. Dramatic doses of chemotherapy racked her body as the oncologists, nurses, and doctors at Vancouver General Hospital placed her on a demanding regimen to save her life. She became very sick, tired, and bald. Her family and faith community stepped up to the plate and grand-slammed world-class love, care, and support for her. As I write, she's leukemia free and alive! Lorna understands what it means to walk courageously through the valley of the shadow of death. She also understands how to practice a magnificent surrender, which releases the riches of living in the Lord. Here's what she posted:

Colossians is filled with the mystery of true wealth. Our riches and inheritance lie in our understanding of the hidden mystery of God in Christ, the hope of glory. As we grasp the rich treasures of wisdom and knowledge hidden in Christ, we will walk worthy, speaking the mystery, bearing fruit in every good work and increasing in the knowledge of God. What a privilege! These riches give strength when we walk through dark valleys, give hope when tomorrow is uncertain, and peace in places of pain. The greatest joy is to hold these treasures of truth as love letters from the One who has "chosen us" and called us "holy and dearly loved." So, "let the Word of Christ richly dwell within you," because Christ is our Life. Lorna.[3]

Dear reader, whatever your situation, whatever your struggle, whatever your success, daily revel in the mystery and majesty of the Lord Jesus Christ. As a surrendered and serving disciple, clothe yourself in him and join his mission in the world, because "you have been given fullness in Christ" (Col 2:10). And "whatever you do, whether in word or deed, do it all in the name of the Lord Jesus, giving thanks to God the Father through him" (Col 3:17).

Like you, I know it's an uphill climb to translate truth into life, from belief to behavior, and from fear to faith. I also know that we can departmentalize our lives into secular and sacred categories. We can live by a dualistic worldview where we consign God and spirituality to the sacred department while we simultaneously consign the rest of life (our workplace, our morality, our social life, and our leisure) to the secular department. This schizophrenic worldview is thoroughly unbiblical, because "when Christ is Lord nothing is secular."[4] Remember, "If Jesus Christ is not Lord of all he is not Lord at all." The next time I sing: "I surrender all," I hope that I'll mean it. I must surrender my heart, mind, emotions, and will to his rule—a commitment to a daily, life-long practice. This also requires that I reform and reorient my identity in Christ to that of a slave and a servant before that of a Christian leader or pastor. I wish I had more space to explore the New Testament metaphors that Paul uses in all his letters to identify what it means to be a disciple of Jesus, submitted to his authority. Scott Bessenecker remarks, "The words *doulos* (slave) or *diakonos* (waiter, servant, or one who performs menial chores) show up in every single letter attributed to Paul in the New Testament as

3. Used by permission.
4. Attributed to John Stott.

pictures of what it means to follow Jesus."[5] Stubborn and self-centered I can be, but slave and servant I must become.

You may want to take some time this week to do a magnificent surrender evaluation of your life. To what extent do you feel you are a slave, and a servant, submitted to Christ Jesus as Lord? As I have, you might want to develop a *rule of life*—a *regula*—that regulates your daily commitment to the first principle, the discipline of surrender. Remember, *the spiritual life is the surrendered life.* Imagine yourself releasing his vast riches, like direct bank deposits, into your life. Perhaps A. W. Tozer's following prayer expresses your restlessness and your request:

> Father, I want to know Thee, but my coward heart fears to give up its toys. I cannot part with them without inward bleeding, and I do not try to hide from Thee the terror of the parting. I come trembling, but I do come. Please root from my heart all those things which have become a very part of my living self, so that Thou mayest enter and dwell there without rival. Then shalt Thou make the place of Thy feet glorious. Then shall my heart have no need of the sun to shine in it, for Thyself wilt be the light of it, and there shall be no night there. In Jesus' Name, Amen.[6]

5. Bessenecker, *How to Inherit the Earth,* 96–97.
6. Tozer, *The Pursuit of God,* 31.

Bibliography

Arndt, Johann. *True Christianity*. Translated By Peter C. Erb. New York: Paulist Press, 1979.

Baillie, John. *A Diary of Private Prayer*. New York: Fireside Books, 1996.

Barclay, William. *The Letters to the Galatians and Ephesians*. Revised ed. The Daily Study Bible Series. Philadelphia: Westminster, 1976.

———. *The Letters to the Philippians, Colossians, and Thessalonians*. Revised ed. The Daily Study Bible Series. Philadelphia: Westminster, 1975.

Bessenecker, Scott A. *How to Inherit the Earth: Submitting Ourselves to a Servant Savior*. Downers Grove: IVP, 2009.

Brooke, Stopford. *The Poetry of Robert Browning*. New Delhi: Atlantic, 2007.

Bunyan, John. *The Pilgrim's Progress: in Today's English*. Retold by James H. Thomas. Chicago: Moody, 1964.

Byrne, Rhonda. *The Secret*. New York: Beyond Words Publishing, 2006.

Carlson, Kent and Mike Lueken. *Renovation of the Church: What Happens When a Seeker Church Discovers Spiritual Formation*. Downers Grove: IVP, 2011.

Chapman, Dom John. *The Spiritual Letters of Dom John Chapman*. London: Sheed & Ward, 1935.

Chittister, Joan. *The Gift of Years: Growing Old Gracefully*. New York: BlueBridge, 2008.

———. *Wisdom Distilled From the Daily: Living the Rule of St. Benedict Today*. HarperSanFrancisco, 1990.

Cory, Lloyd. *Quotable Quotations*. Wheaton: Victor, 1985.

Cox, Harvey. *The Future of Faith*. New York: HarperCollins, 2009.

Dark, David. *The Sacredness of Questioning Everything*. Grand Rapids: Zondervan, 2009.

Derkse, Wil, *The Rule of Benedict for Beginners: Spirituality for Daily Life*. Collegeville: The Liturgical Press, 2003.

Dillard, Annie. *The Writing Life*. New York: HarperPerennial, 1989.

Eliot, T. S. *Christianity and Culture*. San Diego: Harcourt, Brace, 1948.

Fleming, Dean. *Contextualization in the New Testament*. Downers Grove: Intervarsity, 2005.

Foster, Richard. *Celebration of Discipline*. San Francisco: Harper & Row, 1978, 1988.

Goethe von, Johann Wolfgang and Hjalmar Hjorth Boyesen. *Goethe's Works: pt. 1. Wilhelm Meister's Travels*. Philadelphia: George Barrie, 1885.

Grenz, Stanley J. and Roger E. Olson. *Who Needs Theology? An Invitation to the Study of God*. Downers Grove: InterVarsity, 1996.

Grudem, Wayne. *Evangelical Feminism*. Wheaton: Crossway Books, 2006.

Helland, Roger, and Leonard Hjalmarson. *Missional Spirituality: Embodying God's Love From the Inside Out*. Downers Grove: IVP, 2011.

Helland, Roger. *The Journey: Walking With God*. Kent: Sovereign World, 2000.

———. *The Revived Church: A Challenge for Tomorrow's Church Today.* Kent: Sovereign World, 1998.

Hirsch, Alan. *The Forgotten Ways.* Grand Rapids: Brazos, 2006.

Hirsch, Alan with Darryn Altclass, *The Forgotten Ways Handbook: A Practical Guide for Missional Churches.* Grand Rapids: Brazos, 2009.

Hirsch, Alan and Dave Ferguson. *On the Verge: A Journey Into the Apostolic Future of the Church.* Grand Rapids: Zondervan, 2011.

Hirsch, E. D. *Validity in Interpretation.* New Haven: Yale University Press, 1967.

Hughes, R. Kent. *Colossians and Philemon: The Supremacy of Christ.* Preaching the Word Series. Westchester, ILL.: Crossway, 1989.

Hull, Bill. *The Disciple-making Pastor.* Revised ed. Grand Rapids: Baker, 2007.

Lewis, C. S. *Mere Christianity.* New York: Simon & Schuster, 1996.

Little, Paul. *How to Give Away Your Faith.* Downers Grove: InterVarsity, 1966, 1988, 2006.

Lowe, Donna & Kimberly Parker. *Radical Love: Forever Changed.* Sarnia, ONT.: Revival Nation, 2010.

McKnight, Scot. *The King Jesus Gospel: The Original Good News Revisited.* Grand Rapids: Zondervan, 2011.

Moo, Douglas J. *The Letter to the Colossians and to Philemon.* The Pillar New Testament Commentary. Grand Rapids: Eerdmans, 2008.

Murray, Andrew. *Humility.* Fort Washington, PA: Christian Literature Crusade, 1993.

Nouwen, Henri. *With Open Hands.* Notre Dame: Ave Marie Press, 1972, 1995, 2005.

Ortberg, John. *The Me I Want to Be.* Grand Rapids: Zondervan, 2010.

Page, Kirby. *Living Abundantly: A Study of Creative Pioneer Groups Through Twenty-Seven Centuries of Exploration of Pathways To Joyous and Abundant Life.* Toronto: Farrar & Rinehart, 1944.

Peterson, Eugene. *The Jesus Way.* Grand Rapids: Eerdmans, 2007.

———. *Working the Angles: The Shape of Pastoral Integrity.* Grand Rapids, Eerdmans, 1987.

Piper, John. *Let the Nations Be Glad.* 3rd ed. Grand Rapids: Baker Academic, 2010.

Porterfield, Eric. *Sessions with Colossians and Philemon.* Macon: Smyth & Helwys, 2007.

Rule of Benedict. Online: http://www.osb.org/rb/text/toc.html#toc.

Ryle, J. C. *A Call to Prayer.* Online: http://www.anglicanlibrary.org/ryle/sermonsandtracts /calltoprayer.htm.

Sayers, Mark. *The Vertical Self: How Biblical Faith Can Help Us Discover Who We Are in An Age of Self-Obsession.* Nashville: Thomas Nelson, 2010.

Scougal, Henry. *The Life of God in the Soul of Man.* Online: http://www.ccel.org/ccel /scougal/life.i.html.

———. Amazon.com Editorial Review of *The Life of God in the Soul of Man,* by John Piper. Online: http://www.amazon.com/Life-God-Soul-Man/dp/1617201944/ref=sr_1_1 ?s=books &ie=UTF8&qid=1312838039&sr=1-1.

Sweet, Leonard. *Post-Modern Pilgrims.* Nashville: Broadman & Holman, 2000.

Taylor, Dr. and Mrs. Howard. *Hudson Taylor's Spiritual Secret.* OMF International, n.d.

Tolstoy, Leo. *The Kingdom of God is Within You.* London: Oxford University Press, 1936.

Tozer, A. W. *The Pursuit of God.* Harrisburg: Christian Publications, n.d.

Vanhoozer, Kevin J., General ed. *Dictionary for Theological Interpretation of the Bible.* Grand Rapids: Baker Academic, 2005.

Vardy, Peter. *An Introduction to Kierkegaard.* Peabody, MA: Hendrickson, 2008.

Wallis, Jim. *The Call to Conversion.* San Francisco: Harper & Row, 1981.

Walsh, Brian J., and Sylvia C. Keesmaat. *Colossians Remixed.* Downers Grove: IVP Academic, 2004.

Webb, William J. *Slaves, Women & Homosexuals: Exploring the Hermeneutics of Cultural Analysis.* Downers Grove: InterVarsity, 2001.

Wiersbe, Warren. *The Bible Exposition Commentary.* Wheaton: Victor, 1989.

Wikisource. "The Thoughts of the Emperor Marcus Aurelius Antonius." Online: http://en.wikisource.org/wiki/The_Thoughts_of_the_Emperor_Marcus_Aurelius_Antoninus#BOOK_V

Wilkins, Steve, and Mark L. Sanford. *Hidden Worldviews.* Downers Grove: IVP Academic, 2009.

Willard, Dallas. *Renovation of the Heart.* Colorado Springs: NavPress, 2002.

———. *The Spirit of the Disciplines.* New York: Harper & Row, 1988.

Wright, N. T. *Colossians and Philemon.* Tyndale New Testament Commentaries. Leicester: InterVarsity; Grand Rapids: Eerdmans, 1986.

Yancey, Philip. *Prayer: Does it Make a Difference?* Grand Rapids: Zondervan, 2006.

About the Author

Roger B. Helland (ThM, Dallas Theological Seminary; DMin, Trinity Western University) is district executive coach of the Baptist General Conference in Alberta, Canada. Roger has also served as a pastor, Bible college and seminary instructor, church consultant, and seminar speaker. He is the author of numerous articles and four other books: *Missional Spirituality*, *The Journey*, *The Revived Church*, and *Let the River Flow*. He has been a leader in the Vineyard, Mennonite Brethren, Christian and Missionary Alliance, and Baptist traditions.

His mission is to help establish and empower missional, disciple-making leaders and churches. To contact him, visit his website and blog at: http://missionalspirituality.com/